Federal Reserve Bank of New York
Economic Policy Review

Table of Contents

August 1997
Volume 3 Number 3

Special Issue on Inflation Targeting

A Framework for the Pursuit of Price Stability

William J. McDonough
President, Federal Reserve Bank of New York

It is often said that there is a worldwide community of central bankers. I certainly feel that way. Central bankers in all countries share a number of concerns. Perhaps the most important of these is the desire for price stability. While central bankers may differ in the ways they seek to achieve price stability— differences grounded in our respective histories, customs, and institutions—the goal we all strive for is no less important.

Recognizing that no one country's central bank has a monopoly on the right answers, I would like to share with you my views on why I believe price stability is so important and what approaches can be taken to achieve this goal. Before turning to these issues, we must first be clear about what we mean by price stability and how to recognize it when we see it.

In my view, a goal of price stability requires that monetary policy be oriented beyond the horizon of its immediate impact on inflation and the economy. This immediate horizon is on the order of two to three years. This orientation properly puts the focus of a forward-looking policy on the time horizon over which monetary

policy moves today will have their effect and households and businesses will do most of their planning. This is the horizon that is relevant for the definition of price stability articulated by Chairman Greenspan: that price stability exists when inflation is not a consideration in household and business decisions.

A central bank's commitment to price stability over the longer term, however, does not mean that the monetary authorities can ignore the short-term impact of economic events. It is important to recognize that, even if we set ourselves successfully on the path to price stability and even if, as a result, price expectations are contained, we still will not have eliminated all sources of potential inflationary shocks. The reality is that monetary policy can never put the economy exactly where we want it to be.

For example, supply shocks that drive prices up sharply and suddenly—such as the two oil shocks of the 1970s—are always possible. In such an eventuality, the appropriate monetary policy consistent with a goal of price stability would not be to tighten precipitously, but rather to bring inflation down gradually over time, as the economy adjusts to the shift in relative prices. In the event of a shock to the financial system, the appropriate monetary policy might require a temporary reflation.

These comments are based on remarks delivered by Mr. McDonough before the Annual Financial Services Forum of the New York State Bankers Association on March 21, 1996, and the Economic Club of New York on October 2, 1996.

As you can see, I believe that monetary policy must be exercised cautiously. Why do I say this? Because contracts, especially wage contracts, can outlast a good part of, or even exceed, short-term shocks in duration. In the short term, therefore, monetary policy must accept as given the rigidities in wages and prices that these contracts create. Abrupt shifts in policy, given these rigidities, especially a monetary tightening in the face of wages that are unlikely to be cut, can cause unacceptable rises in unemployment and drops in output.

WHY PRICE STABILITY IS SO IMPORTANT AND SO DESIRABLE

In my view, a key principle for monetary policy is that price stability is a means to an end—to promote sustainable economic growth. Price stability is both important and desirable because a rising price level—inflation—even at moderate rates, imposes substantial economic costs on society. All countries incur these costs. They entail, for example:

- increased uncertainty about the outcome of business decisions and profitability;

- negative effects on the cost of capital resulting from the interaction of inflation with the tax system;

- reduced effectiveness of the price and market systems; and

- in particular, distortions that create perverse incentives to engage in nonproductive activities.

Let me be even more explicit about the negative effects of one particular type of nonproductive activity induced by inflation's distortion of incentives—the overinvestment of resources in the financial sector. As a former commercial banker, I am especially aware of the significance of this cost, and I believe that it deserves greater attention than it often receives in economists' lists of the costs of inflation.

The resources in high-inflation economies diverted from productive activities to nonproductive financial transactions are enormous. In the hyperinflations in Europe in the 1920s and again in various emerging market countries in the 1980s, we saw financial sectors grow

severalfold. A number of estimates put the rise in the financial sector share of GDP on the order of 1 percent for every 10 percentage points of inflation up to inflation of about 100 percent. The economies that experienced high inflation consumed more financial transactions for an essentially given amount of real goods and services.

If individuals must spend more time, effort, and resources engaging in financial transactions because of the uncertainty inflation engenders, then more of the economy's productive capacity is transferred to the activity of handling transactions. Clearly, given my background, I am not opposed to an expansion of the financial sector that stems from growth of productivity, growth that offers benefits to the public. Equally clearly, I see an expansion of the financial sector that stems from an increasing number of people employed as middlemen, where none would be needed without the distortion of rising inflation and its attendant uncertainty, as growth that diverts resources better employed elsewhere. A bank branch on every corner means a corner store on none.

In short, the costs of overinvestment in the financial sector, like the costs of all inflation-induced nonproductive activities—such as tax code dodges—decrease the resource base available to the economy for growth. A move to price stability would give these economies the necessary incentives to shift resources back to productive uses. In the case of the financial sector in a high-inflation economy, the transfer of resources to productive uses could be as large as a few percentage points of GDP. This can be serious money indeed. And this is just one of the benefits of regaining price stability.

Rapid moves toward price stability from high inflation, however, do have their costs under certain circumstances. The overdevelopment of a sector for no reason other than the inflation rate is precisely one of those circumstances. The removal of the distortionary incentive—inflation—leads to a rapid transfer of resources out of that sector, causing unemployment and business failures to follow: what was boom, goes bust. In those very same countries where we saw the overexpansion of the financial sector, we have seen the sharp contraction of that sector when inflation was finally brought down. This implies an additional argument for price stability. Namely, in a low-inflation environment, these boom-bust cycles created by distortionary incentives are less likely to emerge and can be more easily contained when they arise.

The avoidance of such unnecessary boom-bust cycles also limits the serious social costs that inflation can impose. For one, inflation may strain a country's social fabric, pitting different groups in a society against each other as each group seeks to make certain its wages keep up with the rising level of prices. Moreover, as we all know, inflation also tends to fall particularly hard on the less fortunate in society, often the last to get employment and the first to lose it. These people do not possess the economic clout to keep their income streams steady, or even buy necessities, when a bout of inflation leads to a boom-bust scenario for the economy. When the bust comes, they also suffer disproportionately.

It is important to note, however, that if we are to set a goal for monetary policy, we must be clear as to what we can expect monetary policy to do and what we know it cannot do. What monetary policy can do is to anchor inflation at low price levels over the long term and thereby lock in inflation expectations. In addition, monetary policy can help offset the effects of financial crises as well as prevent extreme downturns in the economy.

Over the past twenty years, there has been an emerging consensus among policymakers and economists that an activist monetary policy to stimulate output and reduce unemployment beyond its sustainable level leads to higher inflation but not to lower unemployment or higher output. Moreover, although some countries have managed to experience rapid growth in the presence of high inflation rates, often with the help of extensive indexation, none has been able to do so without encountering severe difficulties at a later stage. It is thus widely recognized today that there is no long-run trade-off between inflation and unemployment. As a result, we have witnessed a growing commitment among central banks throughout the world to price stability as the primary goal of monetary policy.

One point is worth emphasizing: Allowing even a low level of inflation to persist without a commitment to bring that level downward toward price stability permits—and may even encourage—expectations for still sharper price rises in the future. Such expectations provide an opening for a demand-driven burst of inflation.

But what monetary policy cannot do, in and of itself, is produce economic growth. Economic growth stems from increases in the supply of capital and labor and from the productivity with which labor and capital are used, neither of which is directly influenced by monetary policy. However, without doubt, monetary policy can help foster economic growth by ensuring a stable price environment.

Some would argue that establishing price stability as the primary goal of monetary policy means that a central bank would no longer be concerned about output or job growth. I would like to make clear for the record that I believe this view to be simply wrong. A stable price and financial environment almost certainly will enhance the capacity of monetary policy to fight occasions of cyclical weakness in the economy. What is important to bear in mind is that by ensuring a stable price environment, monetary policy helps foster economic growth. This is a key point—and is often overlooked.

In trying to determine the extent of future inflation, a central bank must look at a broad array of economic indicators that reflect demand pressures and supply developments in the economy. Unfortunately, there is no single summary measure that provides a reliable overall assessment of the many complex and diverse influences on inflation, which makes it more difficult within most countries to reach a national consensus on policy at any point. Nonetheless, while its one explicit goal must be price stability, monetary policy can and must also maintain the broad environment for sustainable economic growth.

TARGETING FRAMEWORKS FOR MONETARY POLICY

How have central banks sought to achieve price stability? Some countries have begun to commit their central banks statutorily to pursuing the objective of price stability and are granting them a high degree of independence to do so. Empirical research in recent years has shown that both the average rate of inflation and its variability tend to decline in the presence of increased independence for central banks. This is why so many governments, particularly among the emerging market countries, have been providing their central banks with increased autonomy.

Once a commitment has been made to price stability as the goal of monetary policy—and that commitment has been entrusted to an independent central bank—there are several possible approaches to implementing that goal. While the choice will depend on a country's history, economic conditions, and traditions, all successful approaches share two important features: first, they focus on a long-term time horizon and, second, they provide a transparent standard for the assessment of policy. For many of these approaches, what guides monetary policy is an announced target. Such a target is one proven means of credibly conveying to the public the commitment to price stability and thereby locking in inflation expectations.

There are a number of possible targets for monetary policy. All have been used with success in some countries while meeting with failure in others, depending upon the economic context in which they have been implemented. It is useful to step back and review briefly the advantages and drawbacks, as I see them, of three different targeting frameworks—exchange rates, monetary aggregates, and inflation.

Fixing the value of the domestic currency relative to that of a low-inflation country is one approach central banks have used to pursue price stability. The advantage of an exchange rate target is its clarity, which makes it easily understood by the public. In practice, it obliges the central bank to limit money creation to levels comparable to those of the country to whose currency it is pegged. When credibly maintained, an exchange rate target can lower inflation expectations to the level prevailing in the anchor country.

Experiences with fixed exchange rates, however, point to a number of drawbacks. A country that fixes its exchange rate surrenders control of its domestic monetary policy. It can neither respond to domestic shocks that are not felt by the anchor country nor avoid shocks transmitted by the anchor country. Moreover, in the environment of open, global capital markets, fixed exchange rate regimes are subject to sudden speculative attacks when markets perceive that domestic needs and exchange commitments diverge. These speculative attacks can be very disruptive to any country's economy.

On balance, it seems that a fixed exchange rate approach to price stability makes most sense when the country adopting it has an economy closely tied to the country or countries it is pegging to and is thus subject to similar international shocks in any case. This approach could also be worthwhile if a country is unable—for whatever reason—to make a credible commitment to price stability on a domestic basis alone. In either situation, the country must have available a larger, low-inflation anchor country to which it can peg its currency.

Targeting monetary aggregates is another approach many central banks used in the 1970s and 1980s. This approach has been successfully maintained by a few prominent countries. Given a dependable relationship between the targeted monetary aggregate and the goal of price stability—where movement in the monetary aggregate predicts movement in prices—this framework offers a number of advantages. Like exchange rate targeting, an announced monetary target is easily understood by the public. In fact, it conveys more information than an exchange rate target because it shows where monetary policy is and where inflation is likely to be going. The targeting of monetary aggregates has the additional advantage of focusing policy on a quantity that a central bank can control quickly, easily, and directly.

It is important to emphasize that the advantages of a monetary aggregate target are totally dependent upon the predictability of the relationship between the money target and the inflation goal. If fluctuations in the velocity of money—perhaps due to financial innovation—weaken this relationship, this framework will not bring price stability. In the United States, these relationships are not sufficiently stable for the monetary targeting approach to work.

A third approach to price stability is to target inflation. This approach has been adopted by a number of central banks over the past several years, as the following study shows, and the initial results appear positive. The advantage inflation targeting shares with exchange rate and monetary targeting is its transparency to the public. The commitment to price stability is made clear in policy terms, and deviations from the pursuit of the inflation target over the longer term are obvious. Like a monetary aggregate target, an inflation target also provides monetary policy with the necessary flexibility to respond to economic needs in the short term. Finally, targeting inflation avoids the problem of velocity shocks because monetary policy is no longer dependent upon the money-inflation relationship.

The main drawback of inflation targeting is that inflation itself is not directly or even easily controllable by the monetary authorities. Furthermore, policy moves in pursuit of the inflation target only take effect with a lag, so that success in hitting the target is not quickly apparent. This is a problem that is not present in either exchange rate or monetary aggregate targeting. These difficulties may mean that the target cannot strictly be met at times, which, at a minimum, could lead to a rise in inflation expectations. Nevertheless, for countries that are unable or unwilling to fix their exchange rate to that of another country and cannot rely on stable relationships between monetary aggregates and goals, the inflation target approach offers a transparent means of commitment over the longer term. I believe that the inflation-targeting approach to price stability merits further study and consideration.

What a Strategy for Monetary Policy Requires

In my view, therefore, the challenge to monetary policy in today's environment is to consider how we may most effectively build on our current low inflation by making its permanence a credible policy goal. This goal raises a host of important questions.

For one, even if we agree—as I believe we already do—that price stability must be the primary long-term goal of monetary policy, what exactly does price stability mean in practical terms over both the intermediate and long term? Second, what kind of institutional structure is needed to enable the central bank to convey to the markets and the public an explicit commitment to price stability? A related question is how should such a policy be articulated to the public to make the central bank accountable and to foster a political consensus in support of this commitment? Finally, how can an explicit policy commitment to price stability be implemented in practice without pushing the economy too hard in one direction or another? These are a few of the questions we at the Federal Reserve Bank of New York are asking ourselves as we consider the merits of our country's taking a step further in its conduct of monetary policy.

Let me offer two possible basic definitions whose relevance depends on the time frame with which policymakers are concerned. One definition would apply over the long term. In this time frame, as I stated at the outset, I would define price stability as being reached when inflation is not a consideration in household and business decisions.

What does this mean in practice? We know that, as currently measured, a zero inflation rate is not the same thing as price stability. This is because of well-known errors in measuring inflation that stem from many factors, including how quality improvements and new products are valued in the consumer price index. Although there is much research on this topic, economists and policymakers cannot agree upon a single number for the magnitude of this measurement error. In most studies, the error has been estimated to range from 0.5 percent to 2.0 percent. Therefore, as a practical matter, price stability may best be thought of as an inflation rate falling somewhere within this range.

Were we to move to a monetary policy strategy that has a numerical inflation goal, given the problems with measurement error, how might this goal be set? If the inflation goal is set too high, we run the risk of allowing the start of an upward spiral in inflation expectations and inflation. Indeed, this is why I do not believe that price stability is consistent with the 3 percent inflation rate we currently have in the United States.

If, on the other hand, the inflation goal is set too low, we run the risk of tipping the economy into a deflation in which the true price level is actually falling. History has shown that deflation can be extremely harmful to the economy in general, and to financial markets in particular. The worst financial crises in our history have been associated with deflationary periods.

Therefore, were we to set a numerical inflation goal for monetary policy, I believe that an appropriate number for this goal should be within the reasonable range of measurement error—but in the upper end of the range because of the dangers of deflation. Such a numerical goal could be understood as the premium needed to prevent the economy from being tipped toward deflation or needlessly forgoing output.

Thus, in the long term, a numerical definition for price stability would provide a framework for the discussion and evaluation of monetary policy. In practical terms, this would mean that the Federal Reserve would be held accountable to—and when successful, judged credible by—an explicit inflation performance standard that would ensure stable inflation expectations.

In the intermediate term, by contrast, over a period of, say, three years—the time horizon over which monetary policy affects inflation—the goal of monetary policy is to put the economy on the path that moves it toward long-term price stability, taking into account the economic and financial pressures on the economy. At low levels of inflation, there are substantial risks to the economy from driving out the remaining inflation too quickly. In the current environment, therefore, the path for monetary policy in the intermediate term would have to be gradual.

Such an effort might require the numerical inflation goal to sometimes be above the long-term goal for a period of time, but then to trend downward toward the long-term goal. In practice, this means that even though the intermediate policy goal would change, the underlying strategy and the long-term goal of price stability would remain the same.

This gradual and forward-looking strategy is essentially the course that the Federal Reserve has been following over the past several years. Integral to this course have been increased efforts toward greater transparency in the conduct of monetary policy. The announcement of changes in policy at the conclusion of Federal Open Market Committee (FOMC) meetings is evidence of these efforts.

What, then, might be some of the advantages of further increasing transparency by committing the Federal Reserve to an explicit inflation goal? For one, were the Federal Reserve to formalize its strategy by announcing specific intermediate and long-term goals for price stability, it might reduce uncertainty about policy. Moreover, the Federal Reserve could clarify why specific policy moves were made at specific times, with reference to its numerical intermediate-term goal.

In addition, an explicit commitment to price stability and specific numerical goals for inflation could help lock in low inflation expectations, making future inflations and disinflations less likely. Lastly, I believe that, were the Federal Reserve to move to the articulation of such a strategy, public discussion and evaluation of monetary policy would be directed to a tighter, less contentious framework than that which currently exists. This is because the performance of the Federal Reserve in fulfilling its monetary responsibilities would be the issue, while the goals would be unambiguous and well established.

The institutional framework to implement such a strategy is, of course, a question. I believe that the mandate for price stability is of sufficient importance to society that it should be set by the legislative process. Were such an approach to be formalized, the Federal Reserve could articulate its strategy as it currently does under the Humphrey-Hawkins law, or Congress might choose to replace the Humphrey-Hawkins law. The fundamental point is that once numerical inflation goals were set, it would be logical and useful to create some kind of an institutional framework for the Federal Reserve to report its progress in meeting its monetary policy goals.

THE NEED FOR DEBATE ON MONETARY POLICY STRATEGY

I am pleased to share these thoughts with you, encouraged as I am by favorable developments in monetary policy and the credibility I believe the Federal Reserve has earned these past several years in controlling prices while encouraging both growth of the real economy and financial system stability. The discussion of the appropriate strategy for monetary policy and what it might mean in practice is currently an intellectual one, although, I hasten to add, one not confined to ivory towers. This is why we are studying these issues at the Federal Reserve Bank of New York.

Public debate about these issues has begun, and certainly there are many points of view to listen to and evaluate. My remarks and the study that follows are intended to contribute to and help stimulate such discussions. The perspective adopted in the following study, after a review of a variety of experiences in other countries, is generally favorable toward explicit inflation targets. But I recognize that this is a difficult and complex subject, that the value of such targets may not be the same in every country and at all times, and that others may see benefits in alternative approaches to monetary policy. If my remarks and the study provoke further debate on these important issues at the heart of monetary policy and our nation's economic welfare, I will consider our efforts to be a success.

Inflation Targeting: Lessons from Four Countries

Frederic S. Mishkin and Adam S. Posen

Introduction

The key issue facing central banks as we approach the end of the twentieth century is what strategy to pursue in the conduct of monetary policy. One choice of monetary strategy that has become increasingly popular in recent years is inflation targeting, which involves the public announcement of medium-term numerical targets for inflation with a commitment by the monetary authorities to achieve these targets. This study examines the experience in the first three countries that have adopted such an inflation-targeting scheme—New Zealand, Canada, and the United Kingdom—as well as in Germany, which adopted many elements of inflation targeting even earlier. Through close examination of the

experience with inflation targeting, both how targeting operates and how these economies have performed since its adoption, we seek to obtain a perspective on what elements of inflation targeting work as a strategy for the conduct of monetary policy.[1]

Before looking in detail at the individual experiences of these countries, we first discuss the rationale for inflation targeting and the design issues that arise in implementing an inflation-targeting strategy. Then, after the case studies of the individual countries, we provide some preliminary evidence on the effectiveness of inflation targeting in these countries and conclude with an assessment of the inflation-targeting experience.

This study is part of a larger project on inflation targeting with Ben Bernanke and Thomas Laubach. We thank Ben Bernanke, Donald Brash, Kevin Clinton, John Crow, Peter Fisher, Charles Freedman, Andrew Haldane, Neal Hatch, Otmar Issing, Mervyn King, Thomas Laubach, William McDonough, Michel Peytrignet, Georg Rich, and Erich Sporndli for their helpful comments. We are grateful to Laura Brookins for research assistance. The views expressed in the study are those of the authors and not necessarily those of the Federal Reserve Bank of New York, the Federal Reserve System, Columbia University, the National Bureau of Economic Research, or the Institute for International Economics.

Frederic S. Mishkin is Director of Research and Executive Vice President at the Federal Reserve Bank of New York, on leave from the Graduate School of Business, Columbia University, and Research Associate at the National Bureau of Economic Research. Adam S. Posen is Research Associate at the Institute for International Economics, on leave from the International Research Function of the Federal Reserve Bank of New York's Research and Market Analysis Group.

Part I.   The Rationale for Inflation Targeting

The decision to organize a country's monetary strategy around the direct targeting of inflation rests upon a number of economic arguments about what monetary policy can and cannot do. Over the last twenty years, a consensus has been emerging in the economics profession that activist monetary policy to stimulate output and reduce unemployment beyond their sustainable levels leads to higher inflation but not to persistently lower unemployment or higher output. Thus, the commitment to price stability as the primary goal for monetary policy has been spreading throughout the world. Along with actual events, four intellectual developments have led the economics profession to this consensus.

WHY PRICE STABILITY?

The first intellectual development challenging the use of an activist monetary policy to stimulate output and reduce unemployment is the finding, most forcefully articulated by Milton Friedman, that the effects of monetary policy have long and variable lags.[1] The uncertainty of the timing and the size of monetary policy effects makes it very possible that attempts to stabilize output fluctuations may not have the desired results. In fact, activist monetary policy can at times be counterproductive, pushing the economy further away from equilibrium, particularly when the stance of monetary policy is unclear to the public and even to policymakers. This lack of clarity makes it very difficult for policymakers to successfully design policy to reduce output and unemployment fluctuations.[2]

The second development is the general acceptance of the view that there is no long-run trade-off between inflation and unemployment.[3] The so-called Phillips curve relationship illustrates the empirical regularity that a lower unemployment rate or higher output can be achieved in the short run by expansionary policy that leads to higher inflation. As prices rise, households and businesses spend and produce more because they temporarily believe themselves to be better off as a result of higher nominal wages and profits, or because they perceive that demand in the economy is growing. In the long run, however, the rise in output or decline in unemployment cannot persist because of capacity constraints in the economy, while the rise in inflation can persist because it becomes embedded in price expectations. Thus, over the long run, attempts to exploit the short-run Phillips curve trade-off only result in higher inflation, but have no benefit for real economic activity.

The third intellectual development calling into question the use of an activist monetary policy to stimulate output and reduce unemployment is commonly referred to as the *time-inconsistency problem* of monetary policy.[4] The time-inconsistency problem stems from the view that wage- and price-setting behavior is influenced by expectations of future monetary policy. A frequent starting point for discussing policy decisions is to assume that private sector expectations are given at the time policy is made. With expectations fixed, policymakers know they can boost economic output (or lower unemployment) by pursuing monetary policy that is more expansionary than expected. As a result, policymakers who have a stronger interest in output than in inflation performance will try to produce monetary policy that is more expansionary than expected. However, because workers and firms make decisions about wages and prices on the basis of their expectations about policy, they will recognize the policymakers' incentive for expansionary monetary policy and so will raise their expectations of inflation. As a result, wages and prices will rise.

The outcome, in these time-inconsistency models, is that policymakers are actually unable to fool workers and firms, so that on average output will not be higher under such a strategy; unfortunately, however, inflation will be. The time-inconsistency problem suggests that a central bank actively pursuing output goals may end up with a bias to high inflation with no gains in output. Consequently, even though the central bank believes itself to be operating in an optimal manner, it ends up with a sub-optimal outcome.

McCallum (1995b) points out that the time-inconsistency problem by itself does not imply that a central bank will pursue expansionary monetary policy that leads to inflation. Simply by recognizing the problem that forward-looking expectations in the wage- and price-setting process create for a strategy of pursuing unexpectedly expansionary monetary policy, central banks can decide not to play that game. Nonetheless, the time-inconsistency literature points out both why there will be pressures on central banks to pursue overly expansionary monetary policy and why central banks whose commitment to price stability is in doubt can experience higher inflation.

A fourth intellectual development challenging the use of an activist monetary policy to stimulate output and reduce unemployment unduly is the recognition that price stability promotes an economic system that functions more efficiently and so raises living standards. If price stability does not persist—that is, inflation occurs—the society suffers several economic costs. While these costs tend to be much larger in economies with high rates of inflation (usually defined to be inflation in excess of 30 percent a year), recent work shows that substantial costs arise even at low rates of inflation.

The cost that first received the attention of economists is the so-called shoe leather cost of inflation—the cost of economizing on the use of non-interest-bearing money (see Bailey [1956]). The history of prewar central Europe makes us all too familiar with the difficulties of requiring vast and ever-rising quantities of cash to conduct daily transactions. Unfortunately, hyperinflations have occurred in emerging market countries within the last decade as well. Given conventional estimates of the interest elasticity of money and the real interest rate when inflation is zero, this cost is quite low for inflation rates less than 10 percent, remaining below 0.10 percent of GDP. Only when inflation rises to above 100 percent do these costs become appreciable, climbing above 1 percent of GDP (Fischer 1981).

Another cost of inflation related to the additional need for transactions is the overinvestment in the financial sector induced by inflation. At the margin, opportunities to make profits by acting as a middleman on normal transactions, rather than investing in productive activities, increase with instability in prices. A number of estimates put the rise in the financial sector share of GDP on the order of 1 percentage point for every 10 percentage points of inflation up to an inflation rate of 100 percent (English 1996). The transfer of resources out of productive uses elsewhere in the economy can be as large as a few percentage points of GDP and can even be seen at relatively low or moderate rates of inflation.

The difficulties caused by inflation can also extend to decisions about future expenditures. Higher inflation increases uncertainty about both relative prices and the future price level, which makes it harder to arrive at the appropriate production decisions. For example, in labor markets, Groshen and Schweitzer (1996) calculate that the loss of output due to inflation of 10 percent (compared with a level of 2 percent) is 2 percent of GDP. More broadly, the uncertainty about relative prices induced by inflation can distort the entire pricing mechanism. Under inflationary conditions, the risk premia demanded on savings and the frequency with which prices are changed increase. Inflation also alters the relative attractiveness of real versus nominal assets for investment and short-term versus long-term contracting.[5]

The most obvious costs of inflation at low to moderate levels seem to come from the interaction of the tax system with inflation. Because tax systems are rarely indexed for inflation, an increase in inflation substantially raises the cost of capital, causing investment to drop below its optimal level. In addition, higher taxation, which results from inflation, causes a misallocation of capital to different sectors, which in turn distorts the labor supply and leads to inappropriate corporate financing decisions. Fischer (1994) calculates that the social costs from the tax-related distortions of inflation amount to 2 to 3 percent of GDP at an inflation rate of 10 percent. In a recent paper, Feldstein (1997) estimates this cost to be even higher: he calculates the cost of an inflation rate of 2 percent rather than zero to be 1 percent of GDP.

The costs of inflation outlined here decrease the level of resources productively employed in an economy, and thereby the base from which the economy can grow. Mounting evidence from econometric studies shows that, at high levels, inflation also decreases the rate of growth of economies. While time series studies of individual countries over long periods and cross-national comparisons of growth rates are not in total agreement, the consensus is that, on average, a 1 percent rise in inflation can cost an economy 0.1 to 0.5 percentage points in its rate of growth (Fischer 1993). This result varies greatly with the level of inflation—the effects are usually thought to be much greater at higher levels.[6] However, a recent study has presented evidence that the inflation variability usually associated with higher inflation has a significant negative effect on growth even at low levels of inflation, in addition to and distinct from the direct effect of inflation itself.[7]

The four lines of argument outlined here lead the vast majority of central bankers and academic monetary economists to the view that price stability should be the primary long-term goal for monetary policy.[8] Furthermore, to avoid the tendency to an inflationary bias produced by the time-inconsistency problem (or uncertainty about monetary policy goals more generally), monetary policy strategy often relies upon a nominal anchor to serve as a target that ties the central bank's hands so it cannot pursue (or be pressured into pursuing) a strategy of raising output with unexpectedly expansionary monetary policy. As we will see, this anchor need not preclude clearly delineated short-term reactions to financial or significant output shocks in order to function as a constraint on inflationary policy over the long term. A number of potential nominal anchors for monetary strategy can serve as targets.

CHOICE OF TARGETS

One nominal anchor used by almost all central banks at one time or another is a target growth path for a monetary aggregate such as the monetary base or M1, M2, or M3. If velocity is either relatively constant or predictable, a growth target of a monetary aggregate can keep nominal income on a steady growth path that leads to long-term price stability. In such an environment, choosing a monetary aggregate as a nominal anchor has several advantages. First, some monetary aggregates, the narrower the better, can be controlled both quickly and easily by the central bank. Second, monetary aggregates can be measured quite accurately with short lags (in the case of the United States, for example, measures of the monetary aggregates appear within two weeks). Third, as pointed out in Bernanke and Mishkin (1992), because an aggregate is known so quickly, using it as a nominal anchor greatly increases the transparency of monetary policy, which can have important benefits. A monetary aggregate sends almost immediate signals to both the public and the markets about the stance of monetary policy and the intentions of policymakers, thereby helping to fix inflation expectations. In addition, the transparency of a monetary aggregate target makes the central bank more accountable to the public to keep inflation low, which can help reduce pressures on the central bank to pursue expansionary monetary policy.

Although the targeting of monetary aggregates has many important advantages in principle, in practice these advantages come about only if the monetary aggregates have a highly predictable relationship with nominal income. Unfortunately, in many countries, velocity fluctuations have been so large and frequent in the last fifteen years that the relationships between monetary aggregates and goal variables have broken down. Some observers have gone so far as to argue that attempts to exploit these relationships have been a cause of their breakdown. As a result, the use of monetary aggregate targets as a nominal anchor has become highly problematic, and many countries that adopted monetary targets in the 1970s abandoned them in the 1980s. Not surprisingly, many policymakers have been looking for alternative nominal anchors.

Another frequently used nominal anchor entails fixing the value of the domestic currency relative to that of a low-inflation country, say Germany or the United States, or, alternatively, putting the value of the domestic currency on a predetermined path vis-à-vis the foreign currency in a variant of this fixed exchange rate regime known as a crawling peg. The exchange rate anchor has the advantage of avoiding the time-inconsistency problem by precommitting a country's central bank so that it cannot pursue an overly expansionary monetary policy that would lead to a devaluation of the exchange rate. In addition, an exchange rate anchor helps reduce expectations that inflation will approach that of the country to which its currency is pegged. Perhaps most important, an exchange rate anchor is a monetary policy strategy that is easily understood by the public.

As forcefully argued in Obstfeld and Rogoff (1995), however, a fixed exchange rate regime is not without its costs and limitations. With a fixed exchange rate regime, a country no longer exercises control over its own monetary policy. Not only is the country unable to use monetary policy to respond to domestic shocks, but it is also vulnerable to shocks emanating from the country to which its currency is pegged. Furthermore, in the current environment of open, global capital markets, fixed exchange rate regimes are subject to breakdowns that may entail sharp changes in exchange rates. Such developments can be very disruptive to a country's economy, as recent events in Mexico have demonstrated. Defending the domestic currency when it is under pressure may require substantial increases in interest rates that directly cause a contraction in consumer and investment spending, and the contraction in turn may lead to a recession. In addition, as pointed out in Mishkin (1996), a sharp depreciation of the domestic currency can produce a full-scale banking and financial crisis that can tip a country's economy into a severe depression.

An inflation target (or its variant, a price-level target) clearly provides a nominal anchor for the path of the price level, and, like a fixed exchange rate anchor, has the important advantage of being easily understood by the public. The resulting transparency increases the potential for promoting low inflation expectations, which helps to produce a desirable inflation outcome. Also, like a fixed exchange rate or a monetary targeting strategy, inflation targeting reduces the pressure on the monetary authorities to pursue short-run output gains that would lead to the time-inconsistency problem. An inflation-targeting strategy also avoids several of the problems arising from monetary targeting or fixed exchange rate strategies. For example, in contrast to a fixed exchange rate system, inflation targeting can preserve a country's independent monetary policy so that the monetary authorities can cope with domestic shocks and help insulate the domestic economy from foreign shocks. In addition, inflation targeting can avoid the problem presented by velocity shocks because it eliminates the need to focus on the link between a monetary aggregate and nominal income; instead, all relevant information may be brought to bear on forecasting inflation and choosing a policy response to achieve a desirable inflation outcome.

Inflation targeting does have some disadvantages. Because of the uncertain effects of monetary policy on inflation, monetary authorities cannot easily control inflation. Thus, it is far harder for policymakers to hit an inflation target with precision than it is for them to fix the exchange rate or achieve a monetary aggregate target. Furthermore, because the lags of the effect of monetary policy on inflation are very long—typical estimates are in excess of two years in industrialized countries—much time must pass before a country can evaluate the success of monetary policy in achieving its inflation target. This problem does not arise with either a fixed exchange rate regime or a monetary aggregate target.

Another potential disadvantage of an inflation target is that it may be taken literally as a rule that precludes any concern with output stabilization. As we will see in the cases later in our study, this has not occurred in practice. An inflation target, if rigidly interpreted, might lead to greater output variability, although it could lead to tighter control over the inflation rate. For example, a negative supply shock that raises the inflation rate and lowers output would induce a tightening of monetary policy to achieve a rigidly enforced inflation target. The result, however, would add insult to injury because output would decline even further. By contrast, in the absence of velocity shocks, a monetary aggregate target is equivalent to a target for nominal income growth, which is the sum of real output growth and inflation. Because the negative supply shock reduces real output as well as raises the price level, its effect on nominal income growth would be less than on inflation, thus requiring less tightening of monetary policy.

The potential disadvantage of an inflation-targeting regime that ignores output stabilization has led some economists to advocate the use of a nominal income growth target instead (for example, see McCallum [1995a] and Taylor [1995]). A nominal income growth target shares many characteristics with an inflation target; it also has many of the same advantages and disadvantages. On the positive side, it avoids the problems of velocity shocks and the time-inconsistency problem and allows a country to maintain an independent monetary policy. On the negative side, nominal income is not easily controllable by the monetary authorities, and much time must pass before assessment of monetary policy's success in achieving the nominal income target is possible. Still, a nominal growth target is advantageous in that it explicitly includes some weight on a real output objective and thus may lead to smaller fluctuations in real output.[9]

Nonetheless, nominal income targets have two very important disadvantages relative to inflation targets. First, a nominal GDP target forces the central bank or the government to announce a number for potential GDP growth. Such an announcement is highly problematic because estimates of potential GDP growth are far from precise and they change over time. Announcing a specific number for potential GDP growth may thus indicate a certainty that policymakers may not have and may also cause the public to mistakenly believe that this estimate is actually a fixed target. Announcing a potential GDP growth number is, therefore, likely to create an extra layer of political complication—it opens policymakers to the criticism that they are willing to settle for growth rates that are too low. Indeed, it may lead to the accusation that the central bank or the targeting regime is antigrowth, when the opposite is true—that is, a low inflation rate is a means to promote a healthy economy that can experience high growth. In addition, if the estimate for potential GDP growth is too high and it becomes embedded in the public mind as a target, the classic time-inconsistency problem—and a positive inflation bias—will arise.

The second disadvantage of a nominal GDP target relative to an inflation target is that the concept of nominal GDP is not readily understood by the public, thus making it less transparent than an inflation target. No one speaks of "headline nominal GDP growth" when discussing labor contracts. In addition, because nominal and real GDP can be easily confused, a nominal GDP target may lead the public to believe that a central bank is targeting real GDP growth, with the attendant problems mentioned above.

Part II.   Design Issues in the Implementation of Inflation Targets

Part I has outlined the reasons why several countries have chosen to base their monetary strategies on the targeting of inflation. It also raises a set of issues about the design of an inflation-targeting regime. Before examining in detail how inflation targeting has worked in the countries we examine here, we briefly outline the choices policymakers face in designing an inflation-targeting strategy. The fundamental question is how best to balance transparency with flexibility in operation, given the uncertainties of monetary policy and the economic environment. The simpler and tighter the constraints on policy, the easier it is for the public to understand and hold policy accountable, but the harder it is for policy to respond to events and maintain credible performance. Choices about target design are therefore critical in setting this balance appropriately.

In the case studies that follow, we will see that the design choices for an inflation-targeting regime fall into four basic categories: definition and measurement of the target, transparency, flexibility, and timing.

DEFINITION AND MEASUREMENT OF THE TARGET

Because inflation targeting by its very nature requires a numerical value for the target, setting such a target requires explicit answers to several questions about how the target is defined and measured.

What does price stability mean in practice? Inflation targeting requires a quantitative statement as to what inflation rate is consistent with the pursuit of price stability in the next few years. Because of innovation and changing tastes, all inflation measures have a net positive bias. For example, measurement error for consumer price index (CPI) inflation in the United States has been estimated to be in the range of 0.5 to 2.0 percent at an annual rate (Shapiro and Wilcox 1996; Advisory Commission to Study the Consumer Price Index 1996). Another factor to be taken into account in setting the target level of inflation is the asymmetric dangers from deflation. That is, through financial and other channels, the costs to the real economy from undershooting zero inflation outweigh the direct costs to the economy from overshooting zero inflation by a similar amount. These potential costs might warrant a price stability objective in which the inflation rate, corrected for any measurement error, might be set slightly above zero.

What inflation series should be targeted and who should measure it? A target series must be defined and measured. The series needs to be considered accurate, timely, and readily understandable by the public, but it may also need to exclude from its definition individual price shocks or one-time shifts that do not affect trend inflation, which is what monetary policy can influence.

Price-level or inflation target? Both price-level and inflation targets imply a targeted path for the price level. A price-level target sets the path for the price level so that if inflation is above the targeted rate in one period, it must be below the targeted rate in the next period in order to hit the price-level target. By contrast, an inflation target allows for "base drift," in which bygones are bygones, and the miss on the inflation target does not need to be offset. Relative to an inflation target, a price-level target has the advantage of helping to pin down price-level expectations over very long time horizons, but it may increase the volatility of the price level over shorter time horizons.

TRANSPARENCY

An important rationale for inflation targeting is that it promotes transparency in monetary policy. Two questions need to be answered if transparency is to be achieved.

How should inflation targets be used to communicate with the public and the markets? Inflation targets can be an effective way of increasing transparency by communicating information to the public and the markets about the stance and intentions of monetary policy. A variety of institutional arrangements, published materials, testimony, and speeches can help in this communication process and can emphasize the forward-looking nature of monetary policy. In addition, clear, regular explanations of monetary policy by central banks can build public support for and understanding of the pursuit of price stability.

How should central banks be held accountable for target performance? Because monetary policy has such important effects on the public, inflation targeting cannot be done without democratic accountability. The extent to which this accountability takes the form of structured discussion rather than political pressure can in part be determined by target design. Who should set the inflation target: the government, the central bank, or both together?

FLEXIBILITY

As McDonough (1996a) suggests, price stability is a means to an end—the creation of a stable economic environment that promotes economic growth—rather than an end in itself. Control over inflation that is too tight might be costly in terms of higher output variability. Thus, the design of an inflation-targeting regime must answer questions about how much flexibility should be built into it.

What deviations from the inflation target should be allowed in response to shocks? As the discussion of the merits of an inflation

target versus a nominal income growth target suggests, a rigid inflation target may not be sufficiently flexible in response to some shocks. Because both policymakers and the public care about output fluctuations, and the ultimate reason for price stability is to support a healthy real economy, an inflation-targeting regime may need escape clauses or some flexibility built into the target definition to deal with supply and other types of shocks.

Should the target be a point or a range? Because of shocks to the inflation process and uncertainty about the effects of monetary policy, inflation outcomes will have a high degree of uncertainty even with the best monetary policy settings. Should an inflation target have a range to allow for this uncertainty? Estimates of this uncertainty are quite high (see, for example, Haldane and Salmon [1995] and Stevens and Debelle [1995]), and so an inflation target band would have to be quite wide—on the order of 5 or 6 percentage points—in order to allow for this uncertainty. However, a band this wide might cause the public and the markets to doubt the central bank's commitment to the inflation target. An alternative approach is a point target, which—in order to address the uncertainties of inflation outcomes—would be accompanied by discussion of the shocks that might drive inflation away from the target goal.

Should inflation targets be varied over time? If there is substantial inertia in the wage- and price-setting process and inflation is initially very high, the monetary authorities might want to avoid a rapid transition to the price stability goal. In this case, they might well choose a transition path of inflation targets that trends downward over time, toward the price stability goal. Similarly, even if the price stability goal were achieved, shocks to the economy might move the economy away from this goal, again raising the issue of whether the inflation targets should be varied over time. Varying inflation targets over time may thus be used as another tool to increase the flexibility of the inflation-targeting regime so that it can cope with supply and other types of shocks to the economy.

TIMING

Two questions arise with respect to the timing of inflation targets:

What is the appropriate time horizon for an inflation target? Because monetary policy affects inflation with long lags, monetary policy cannot achieve a specific inflation target immediately, but instead achieves its goal over time. Also, economic shocks can occur in the intervening period between policy and effect. Monetary policymakers must thus decide what time horizon is appropriate for meeting the inflation target.

When is the best time to start implementing inflation targets? To establish credibility for an inflation-targeting regime, it may be important to have some initial successes in achieving the inflation targets. This suggests that certain periods may be better than others to introduce inflation targets. Furthermore, obtaining political support for the commitment to price stability underlying an inflation-targeting regime may be easier at certain times than at others, so choosing the correct time to implement inflation targeting may be an important element in its success or failure.

CASE STUDIES

We will see that these four categories of decisions about operational design are recurring themes in the case study discussions that follow. What is striking is the extent to which a number of the target-adopting countries have converged on a few design choices, perhaps indicating an emerging consensus on best practices.

The case studies are structured as follows. The first section outlines why and under what circumstances the targeting regime was adopted. The next section describes the operational framework of the targeting regime. The third section describes the actual targeting experience. The final section provides a brief summary of the key lessons to be drawn from each country's experience. The case studies begin with Germany because it was one of the first countries (along with Switzerland) to implement many of the features of an inflation-targeting regime, even though Germany is not an inflation targeter per se. Although Germany focuses principally on monetary aggregates as the target variables, there is much to learn from its experience, which has been longer than that of the other countries discussed here. The remaining case studies then proceed according to the order in which the countries adopted inflation targeting: New Zealand, then Canada, and finally the United Kingdom.

Part III.   German Monetary Targeting: A Precursor to Inflation Targeting

Many features of the German monetary targeting regime are also key elements of inflation targeting in the other countries examined in this study. Indeed, as pointed out in Bernanke and Mishkin (1997), Germany might best be thought of as a "hybrid" inflation targeter, in that it has more in common with inflation targeting than with a rigid application of a monetary targeting rule. The German experience with monetary targeting, which spans more than twenty years, provides useful lessons for the successful operation of inflation targeting, and this is why we study the German experience here.

Several themes emerge from our review of Germany's experience with monetary targeting:[1]

- A numerical inflation goal is a key element in German monetary targeting, suggesting that the differences between monetary targeting as actually practiced by Germany and inflation targeting as conducted by other countries are not that great.

- German monetary targeting is quite flexible: convergence of the medium-term inflation goal to the long-term goal has often been quite gradual.

- Under the monetary targeting regime, monetary policy has been somewhat responsive in the short run to real output growth as well as to other considerations such as the exchange rate.

- The long-term goal of price stability has been defined as a measured inflation rate greater than zero.

- A key element of the targeting regime is a strong commitment to transparency and to communication of monetary policy strategy to the general public.

THE ADOPTION OF MONETARY TARGETING

The decision to adopt monetary targeting in Germany, though prompted by the breakdown of the Bretton Woods fixed exchange rate regime, was a matter of choice. Germany was not under any pressure at the time to reform either its economy in general or its monetary regime in particular—in fact, the breakdown of Bretton Woods was in part due to the extreme relative credibility of the German central bank's commitment to price stability and the concomitant appreciation of the deutsche mark. Under these circumstances, the loss of the exchange rate anchor was not the sort of credibility crisis where macroeconomic effects demanded an immediate response, as demonstrated by the slow (two-to-three-year-long) move to the new regime.

Close analysis of the historical record suggests that two main factors motivated the adoption of monetary targeting in Germany. The first factor was an intellectual argument in favor of a nominal anchor for monetary policy grounded in an underlying belief that monetary policy should neither accommodate inflation nor pursue medium-term output goals.[2] The second factor was the perception that medium-term inflation expectations had to be locked in when monetary policy eased as inflation came down after the first oil shock. The generalization over time of this latter motivation—that monetary targeting provides a means of transparently and credibly communicating the relationship between current developments and medium-term goals—was the guiding principle of the newly adopted framework in Germany.

On December 5, 1974, the Central Bank Council of the Deutsche Bundesbank announced that "from the present perspective it regards a growth of about 8% in the central bank money stock over the whole of 1975 as acceptable in the light of its stability goals."[3] The Bundesbank considered this target to "provide the requisite scope . . . for the desired growth of the real economy," while at the same time the target had been chosen "in such a way that no new inflationary strains are likely to arise as a result of monetary developments." Since 1973, the Bundesbank had used the central bank money stock (CBM) as its primary indicator of monetary developments, but never before had it announced a target for the growth of CBM or any other monetary aggregate.[4] Although this was a unilateral announcement on the part of the Bundesbank, the announcement stressed that "in formulating its target for the growth of the central bank money stock [the Bundesbank] found itself in full agreement with the federal government."

Although its statements at the time do not make the point explicitly, one of the Bundesbank's primary concerns appears to have been that public misperceptions might entrench high inflation expectations. At the beginning of 1975, the Bundesbank faced the task of continuing to ease monetary policy in view of the already apparent weakness in the economy, without giving the impression that its resolve to bring down inflation was diminishing. Recent experience had shown that wage-setting behavior in particular was mostly unaffected by the Bundesbank's efforts to reduce inflation:

> Wage costs have gone up steadily in the last few months, partly as after-effects of [earlier] settlements . . . which were excessive (not least because management and labor obviously underestimated the prospects of success of the stabilization policy). . . . Despite the low level of business activity and subdued inflation expectations, even in very recent wage negotiations two-figure rises have effectively been agreed. (Deutsche Bundesbank 1974b, December, p. 6)

The credibility issue arose, therefore, in the context of the Bundesbank's desire to stop the pass-through of a onetime shock to the price level; this concern for getting the public to distinguish between first-round and second-round effects of a price shock and to avoid locking in expectations of high inflation characterizes the efforts of the inflation targeters as well.

From this perspective, the German monetary target seems to have been adopted, at least in part, to create a necessary means of communication about inflation uncertainty. After CBM had grown by 6 percent during 1974, the Bundesbank announced a target growth rate of 8 percent for 1975:

> An acceleration of money growth was intended to stimulate demand and provide the monetary scope necessary for the desired real growth of the economy. On the other hand, the target was also intended to show that no precipitate action would be taken to ease monetary conditions, in order not to jeopardize further progress towards containing the inflationary tendencies. (Deutsche Bundesbank 1976a, p. 5)

It is worth noting, however, that this explanation and the statement cited in the previous paragraph were made *after* the targets were announced, not contemporaneously with the announcement.

THE OPERATIONAL FRAMEWORK

Our historical and institutional analysis in this section and the following one (which discusses German monetary policy in the 1990s) independently confirms the impression of German monetary policymaking raised in Bernanke and Mishkin (1992) and argued by later econometric observers. That is, the Bundesbank does not behave according to a reduced-form-reaction function as though price stability were its sole short-to-medium-term policy goal, or as though the monetary growth–goal correlation were strong enough to justify strictly following the targets, ignoring wider information.[5] In fact, in the following discussion we bring out the operational reality and implications: that the monetary targets provide a framework for the central bank to convey its long-term commitment to price stability.

From 1975 until 1987, the Bundesbank announced targets for the growth of central bank money (CBM). CBM is defined as currency in circulation plus sight deposits, time deposits with maturity under four years, and savings deposits and savings bonds with maturity of less than four years (the latter three components are weighted by their respective required reserve ratios as of January 1974). CBM is different from the monetary base in that banks' excess balances are excluded and the weights of deposits subject to reserve requirements are historical, not current, ratios.

Since 1988, the Bundesbank has used growth in M3 as its intermediate target. M3 is defined as the sum of currency in circulation, sight deposits, time deposits with maturity under four years, and savings deposits at three months' notice. Apart from not including savings deposits with longer maturities and savings bonds, the major difference between M3 and CBM is that the latter is a weighted-sum aggregate, while the former is a simple sum. By definition, therefore, CBM moves very closely with M3. Because the weights on the three types of deposits are fairly small,[6] the only source for large divergences between the growth of the two aggregates is significant fluctuation in the holdings of currency as compared with deposits. This potential divergence became critical in 1988, in the face of shifting financial incentives, and again in 1990-91, after German monetary unification.

The Bundesbank has always set its monetary targets at the end of a calendar year for the next year. It derives the monetary targets from a quantity equation, which states that the amount of nominal transactions in an economy within a given period of time is identically equal to the amount of the means of payment times the velocity at which the means of payment changes hands. In rate-of-change form, the quantity equation states that the sum of real output growth and the inflation rate is equal to the sum of money growth and the change in (the appropriately defined) velocity. The Bundesbank derives the target growth rate of the chosen monetary aggregate (CBM or M3) by estimating the growth of the long-run production potential over the coming year, adding the rate of price change it considers unavoidable (described below), and subtracting the estimated change in trend velocity over the year.

Two elements of this procedure deserve emphasis. First, the Bundesbank does not employ forecasts of real output growth over the coming year in its target derivation, but instead estimates the growth in production potential.[7] This "potential-oriented approach" is based on the Bundesbank's conviction that it should not engage in policies aimed at short-term stimulation. This approach allows the Bundesbank not only to claim that it is not making any choice about the business cycle when it sets policy, but also to de-emphasize any public discussion of its forecasting efforts for the real economy, further distancing monetary policy from the course of unemployment. The transparency of the quantity approach, therefore, gets certain items off the monetary policy agenda (or at least moves in that direction) by specifying the central bank's responsibilities.

The second noteworthy element of the Bundesbank's procedure for deriving the target growth rate of its chosen monetary aggregate relates to the concept of "unavoidable price increases," where prices are measured by the all-items consumer price index (CPI). These goals for inflation are set prior to the monetary target each year and specify the intended path for inflation, which in turn motivates monetary policy.

> In view of the unfavorable underlying situation, the Bundesbank felt obliged until 1984 to include an "unavoidable" rate of price rises in its calculation. By so doing, it took due account of the fact that price increases which have already entered into the decisions of economic agents cannot be eliminated immediately, but only step by step. On the other hand, this tolerated rise in prices was invariably below the current inflation rate, or the rate forecast for the year ahead. The Bundesbank thereby made it plain that, by adopting an unduly "gradualist" approach to fighting inflation, it did not wish to contribute to strengthening inflation expectations. Once price stability was virtually achieved at the end of 1984, the Bundesbank abandoned the concept of "unavoidable" price increases. Instead, it has since then included . . . a medium-term price assumption of 2%. (Deutsche Bundesbank 1995c, pp. 80-1)

The setting of the annual unavoidable price increase thus embodies four normative judgments by the Bundesbank. First, a medium-term goal for inflation motivates policy decisions. Second, convergence of the medium-term goal to the long-term goal should be gradual since the costs of moving to the long-run goal cannot be ignored. Third, the medium-term inflation goal has always been defined as a number greater than zero. Fourth, if inflation expectations remain contained, there is no need to reverse prior price-level rises.

The target for 1975 was a point target for CBM growth from December 1974 to December 1975. Since this target definition was susceptible to short-term fluctuations in money growth around year-end, the targets from 1976 to 1978 were formulated as point targets for the average growth of CBM over the previous year.

In 1979, two changes to the target formulation were made. First, with the exception of 1989, all targets have been formulated in terms of a target range of plus or minus 1 or 1.5 percent around the monetary target derived from the quantity equation.

> In view of the oil price hikes in 1974 and 1979-80, the erratic movements in "real" exchange rates and the weakening of traditional cyclical patterns, it appeared advisable to grant monetary policy from the outset limited room for discretionary maneuver in the form of such target ranges. To ensure that economic agents are adequately informed . . . the central bank must be prepared to define from the start as definitely as possible the overall economic conditions under which it will aim at the top or bottom end of the range. (Schlesinger 1983, p. 10)

In moving to a target range rather than a point target, the Bundesbank believed that, by giving itself room for response to changing developments, it could hit the target range; in fact, the tone of its explanation suggests that it was conferring some discretion upon itself rather than buying room for error in a difficult control problem.

The second change made in 1979 was to reformulate the targets as growth rates of the average money stock in the fourth quarter over the average money stock in the previous year in order to indicate "the direction in which monetary policy is aiming more accurately than an average target does" (Deutsche Bundesbank 1979b, January, p. 8). Chart 3 (p. 34) depicts quarterly growth rates of CBM (through 1987) and M3 (thereafter) over the fourth-quarter level of the previous year and the targets since 1979 (the earlier targets are omitted because they were not formulated in terms of year-on-year rates).

The Bundesbank has repeatedly stressed that situations may arise where it would consciously allow deviations from the announced target path to occur in order to support other economic objectives. These allowances are beyond and in addition to those implicit in the setting of a target range and of a gradual path for movements in unavoidable inflation. A case in point is the year 1977, when signs of weakness in economic activity, combined with a strong appreciation of the deutsche mark, prompted the Bundesbank to tolerate the overshooting of the target. As said at the time:

> However, the fact that the Bundesbank deliberately accepted the risk of a major divergence from its quantitative monetary target does not imply that it abandoned the more medium-term orientation which has marked its policies since 1975. . . . There may be periods in which the pursuit of an "intermediate target variable," as reflected in the announced growth rate of the central bank money stock, cannot be given priority. (Deutsche Bundesbank 1978a, p. 22)

The main reason why CBM was initially chosen as the target aggregate was the Bundesbank's perception of CBM's advantages in terms of transparency and communication to the public. The Bundesbank explained its choice of CBM in the following words:

> [CBM] brings out the central bank's responsibility for monetary expansion especially clearly. The money creation of the banking system as a whole and the money creation of the central bank are closely linked through currency in circulation and the banks' obligation to maintain a certain portion of their deposits with the central bank. Central bank money, which comprises these two components, can therefore readily serve as an indicator of both. A rise by a certain rate in central bank money shows not only the size of the money creation of the banking system but also the extent to which the central bank has provided funds for the banks' money creation. (Deutsche Bundesbank 1976a, p. 12)

Although at any point in time CBM is a given quantity from the Bundesbank's point of view because of the minimum reserve requirements, the choice of CBM nevertheless also reflects the monetary policy stance in the recent past. It is worth noting that this use of CBM to publicly track the monetary stance is consistent with the Bundesbank's focus on having minimum reserve requirements (as seen in the Bank's advocacy of such requirements for the unified European currency). The information being conveyed by CBM in this context, however, is not so much to prevent either the public or the central bank from making a large mistake about the unclear stance of monetary policy (a major concern in the framework design of inflation targeters such as Canada), but to give rapid feedback about the state of monetary conditions in general. The mindset is that monetary control provides useful information about policy and lowers policy uncertainty.

The Bundesbank's confidence that it can explain target deviations and redefinitions to the public is reflected in the design of its reporting mechanisms. There is no legal requirement in the Bundesbank Act or in later legislation for the Bundesbank to give a formal account of its policy to any public body. The independence of the central bank in Germany limits government oversight to a commitment that "the Deutsche Bundesbank shall advise the Federal Cabinet on monetary policy issues of major importance, and shall furnish it with information upon request" (Act Section 13). The only publications that the Bundesbank is required to produce are announcements in the *Federal Gazette* of the setting of interest rates, discount rates, and the like (Act Section 33). According to Act Section 18, the Bundesbank may at its discretion publish the monetary and banking statistics that it collects.

The Bundesbank chooses to make heavy use of this opportunity. On the inside front cover, the *Monthly Report* is described as a response to Section 18 of the Bundesbank Act, but it does much more than report statistics. Every month, after a "Short Commentary" on monetary developments, securities markets, public finance, economic conditions, and the balance of payments, there appear two to four articles on a combination of onetime topics (for example, "The State of External Adjustment after German Reunification") and recurring reports (for example, "The Profitability of German Credit Institutions" [annual] and "The Economic Scene in Germany" [quarterly]). Each year in January, the monetary target and its justification are printed (between 1989 and 1992, the target and justification were available in December). The *Annual Report* gives an extremely detailed retrospective of economic, not just monetary, developments in Germany for the year, lists

all monetary policy moves, and offers commentary on the fiscal policy of the federal government and the *Länder*.[8] Between these two publications, and regularly updated "special publications" such as *The Monetary Policy of the Bundesbank* (an explanatory booklet), no Bundesbank policy decision is left unexplained with respect to both its immediate impact and its short- and long-term effects.

The Bundesbank's commitment to transparency does not come without self-imposed limits on its accountability. Two limitations in particular provide a strong contrast to the inflation report documents prepared by central banks in Canada, the United Kingdom, and other countries in recent years. First, no articles in the *Monthly Report* are signed either individually or collectively by authors, and the *Annual Report* has only a brief foreword signed by the Bundesbank President (although all Council members are listed on the pages preceding it). Speeches by the President or other Council members are never reprinted in either document. This depersonalization of policy is to some extent made up for by the enormously active speaking and publishing schedule that all Council members (not just the President and Chief Economist) and some senior staffers engage in, but the fact of depersonalized reports still weakens the link between the main policy statements and the responsible individuals.

The second limitation on accountability is that the *Monthly Report* and the *Annual Report* always deal with the current situation or assess past performance[9]—no forecasts of any economic variable are made public by the Bundesbank, and private sector forecasts or even expectations are not discussed. The Bundesbank makes itself accountable on the basis of its explanations for past performance, but it does not leave itself open to be evaluated as a forecaster. In fact, its ex post explanations, combined with its potential GDP and normative inflation basis for the monetary targets, enable the Bundesbank to shift responsibility for short-term economic performance to other factors at any time. Nevertheless, those same monetary targets are seen by the Bundesbank as the main source of accountability and transparency because they commit the Bundesbank to explaining policy with respect to a benchmark on a regular basis.

GERMAN MONETARY POLICY UNDER MONETARY TARGETING

The history of the German experience with inflation and monetary targeting up until 1990 has been discussed elsewhere (for example, see Bernanke and Mishkin [1992] and Neumann and von Hagen [1993]). Rather than review the entire history of German monetary targeting, we start by highlighting events through the 1970s and 1980s that are illustrative of certain themes discussed above— particularly the treatment of the monetary targets not as rigid rules but as a means of structured transparency for monetary policy.

Then, the bulk of our discussion focuses on the challenging episode of German monetary unification. In that instance, the Bundesbank successfully handled a (by definition) onetime inflationary shock of great magnitude and politically sensitive developments in the real economy through flexibility and communication. Close examination of this episode also illustrates how the Bundesbank has operated its monetary targeting regime in the 1990s and provides a baseline for the three inflation targeters we examine next. Charts 1-4 (pp. 33-4) track the path of inflation, interest rates, monetary growth, GDP growth, and unemployment before and after monetary union.

It is fair to generalize that in the 1970s and 1980s the Bundesbank frequently over- and undershot its annual monetary targets; it reversed overshootings in most but not all cases. In addition, the Bundesbank responded to movements in other variables besides inflation. From the beginning of CBM targeting in 1975, the Bundesbank was aware of the risk that "central bank money is prone to distortions caused by special movements in currency in circulation" (Deutsche Bundesbank 1976a, p. 11). In 1977, the Bundesbank allowed CBM growth to exceed the target in the face of an appreciating deutsche mark and weak economic activity.[10] At that early time, only two years after the adoption of the targets, the Bundesbank relied on the power of its explanation that "there may be periods in which the pursuit of an 'intermediate target variable' . . . cannot be given priority," acknowledging the importance of intervening real and foreign exchange developments in its decision making (Deutsche Bundesbank 1978a, p. 2).

In 1981 and early 1982, CBM grew much more slowly than M3 because of weakness in the deutsche mark, leading to large-scale repatriation of deutsche mark notes and an inverted yield curve that caused portfolio shifts out of currency into high-yielding short-term assets. Accordingly, the monetary target for 1981 of 4 to 7 percent was undershot (Chart 3, p. 34); since during this period the Bundesbank was pursuing a disinflationary course, and progress was being made on the inflation front, the central bank did not act to bring money growth up into target range.

In 1986 and 1987, the reverse situation—a strong deutsche mark combined with historically low short-term interest rates—led to CBM growth of 7.7 percent and 8 percent, respectively, while M3 grew at 7 percent and 6 percent during those two years, so that all measures exceeded the target monetary growth range. The Bundesbank's allowance of this overshooting could be seen as part of the results of the Plaza Accord on the Group of Seven exchange rates as well. The latter development prompted the Bundesbank to announce a switch in 1988 to monetary targets for the aggregate M3:

> The expansion of currency in circulation is in itself of course a significant development which the central bank plainly has to heed. This is, after all, the most liquid form of money . . . and not least the kind of money which the central bank issues itself and which highlights its responsibility for the value of money. On the other hand, especially at times when the growth rates of currency in circulation and deposit money are diverging strongly, there is no reason to stress the weight of currency in circulation unduly. (Deutsche Bundesbank 1988b, March, "Methodological Notes on the Monetary Target Variable 'M3,'" pp. 18-21)

The fact that the Bundesbank changed the target variable when CBM grew too fast, but did not do so when it grew too slowly, can be interpreted as an indication of the importance that the Bundesbank attaches to the communicative function of its monetary targets. Allowing the target variable to repeatedly overshoot the target because of special factors to which the Bundesbank did not want to react might have led to the misperception on the part of the public that the Bundesbank's attitude toward monetary control and inflation had changed.[11]

An econometric argument has been made by Clarida and Gertler (1997) that the Bundesbank has displayed an asymmetry in reacting to target misses; that is, it usually raises interest rates in response to an overshooting of the target, but it does not lower interest rates in response to an undershooting. In any event, the switch in targeted monetary aggregates was not accompanied by any other alterations in the monetary framework, and the perceived need for the switch did not seem to occasion much concern. In short, as long as the underlying inflation goal was met over the medium term, the existence of the monetary targets rather than their precise functionality was sufficient.

As noted in the previous section's discussion of unavoidable price increases (later termed normative levels of price increase) underlying the Bundesbank's monetary targets, the Bundesbank has tended to pursue disinflation gradually when inflationary shocks occur. The Bundesbank's response to the 1979 oil-induced supply shock was very gradual and publicly stated to be so—the Bundesbank set its level of unavoidable price inflation for 1980 at 8 percent, clearly below the then-prevailing rate, but also clearly above the level of price inflation that was acceptable over the longer term. The target inflation level was brought down in stages, eventually returning to the long-run goal of 2 percent only in 1984. Even though the underlying intent was clear, each year's target unavoidable inflation level (as well as the monetary target and interest rate policies determined by that level) was actually set only a year ahead, allowing the Bundesbank still further flexibility to respond to events and to rethink the pace of disinflation. Although what turned out to be four years of marked inflation reduction is hardly an instance of the Bundesbank going easy on inflation, it is an illustration of flexibility and concern for the real-side economic effects of German monetary policy.

The economic situation in the Federal Republic of Germany during the two years prior to economic and monetary union with the German Democratic Republic (GDR) on July 1, 1990, ("monetary union") was characterized by GDP growth of around 4 percent and the first significant fall in unemployment since the late 1970s (Chart 4, p. 34). After a prolonged period of falling inflation and histori-

cally low interest rates during the mid-1980s, inflation had increased from -1 percent at the end of 1986 to slightly more than 3 percent by the end of 1989. The Bundesbank had begun tightening monetary policy in mid-1988, raising the repo rate in steps from 3.25 percent in June 1988 to 7.75 percent in early 1990. After the first M3 target of 3 to 6 percent had been overshot in 1988 by 1 percent, the target for M3 growth of around 5 percent in 1989 was almost exactly achieved, with M3 growing at 4.7 percent. M3 growth was certainly not high in view of the prevailing rate of economic growth.

In response to the uncertainties resulting from the prospect of German reunification, long-term interest rates had increased sharply from late 1989 until March 1990, with ten-year bond yields rising from around 7 percent to around 9 percent in less than half a year. Combined with a strong deutsche mark, this rise in long-term interest rates allowed the Bundesbank to keep official interest rates unchanged during the months immediately preceding monetary union. In the immediate aftermath of monetary union it kept official interest rates unchanged as well, despite the fact that the effects of the massively expansionary fiscal policy accompanying reunification were beginning to propel GDP growth to record levels.

To some extent, the Bundesbank's decision to keep official interest rates unchanged for the first few months following monetary union was due to the fact that the inflationary potential resulting from the conditions under which the GDR mark had been converted into deutsche marks was very difficult to assess. The Bundesbank had been opposed to the conversion rate agreed to in the treaty on monetary union (on average about 1 to 1.8) and had been publicly overruled on this point by the federal government.[12] The money stock M3 had increased almost 15 percent because of monetary union. The rate of conversion chosen turned out to be almost exactly right. While GDP in the former GDR was estimated to be only around 7 percent of the Federal Republic's once reunification took place, with the vast government transfers to the east all of the money was absorbed (see König and Willeke [1996]). During the first few months following monetary union, the Bundesbank was preoccupied as well with assessing the portfolio shifts in east Germany in response to the introduction not only of a new currency, but also of a new financial system and a broad range of assets that had not previously existed there.

As the east German banks were adjusting to their new institutional structure, and velocity was destabilized by portfolio shifts in east Germany, monetary data that included east Germany were hard to interpret. The Bundesbank therefore continued during the second half of 1990 to calculate monetary aggregates separately for east and west Germany, based on the returns of the banks domiciled in the respective parts. Although M3 growth in west Germany accelerated in late 1990 as a result of the moderate growth rates during the first half of the year, growth of M3 during 1990 of 5.6 percent was well within the target range of 4 to 6 percent.

During the fall of 1990, the repo rate had approached the lombard rate, which meant that banks were increasingly using the lombard facility for their regular liquidity needs and not as the emergency facility for which the Bundesbank intended lombard loans to be used. On November 2, 1990, the Bundesbank raised the lombard rate from 8 to 8.5 percent as well as the discount rate from 6 to 6.5 percent. Within the next few weeks, however, banks bid up the interest rate (*Mengentender*), and the repo rate rose above the lombard rate, prompting the Bundesbank to raise the lombard rate to 9 percent as of February 1, 1991. With these measures, the Bundesbank was reacting to both the volatile GDP growth rates and the faster M3 growth in the last part of 1990. Inflation had until then remained fairly steady, but it seems likely that the Bundesbank at that point was probably expecting inflationary pressures to develop in the near future given the fiscal expansion, the overstretched capacities in west Germany, and the terms of monetary union.

At the end of 1990, the Bundesbank announced a target range for M3 growth of 4 to 6 percent for the year 1991, applying a monetary target for the first time to the whole currency area. The target was based on the average all-German M3 stock during the last quarter of 1990. As this stock was still likely to be affected by ongoing portfolio shifts in east Germany, the target was subject to unusually high uncertainty. It is worth noting that neither the basic inputs into the quantity equation that generates the Bundesbank's money growth targets' normative inflation nor the potential growth rate of the German economy was changed.[13]

> Following German unification, the monetary targets set by the Bundesbank were decidedly ambitious as they left normative inflation, on which these targets are based, unchanged at 2% during this period, even though it was obvious from the outset that this rate could not be achieved in the target periods concerned. (Issing 1995a)

This statement was one of policy—the reunification shock did not fundamentally alter the basic structures of the German economy. Moreover, this statement communicated to the public at large that any price shifts coming from this shock should be treated as a onetime event and not be passed on to inflationary expectations.

This stance required faith in the public's comprehension of, and the Bundesbank's ability to credibly explain, the special nature of the period. It is important to contrast this adherence to the 2 percent medium-term inflation goal with the Bundesbank's response to the 1979 oil shock, when, as already noted, unavoidable inflation was ratcheted up to 8 percent and brought down only slowly. There are two explanations for the difference in policy response in the 1990-93 period, neither of which excludes the other: first, the monetary unification shock was a demand rather than a supply shock, and so the Bundesbank was correct not to accommodate it; and second, after several years of monetary targeting, the Bundesbank's transparent explanations of monetary policy had trained the public to discern the differences between onetime price-level increases and persistent inflationary pressures. In any event, the Bundesbank was clearly allowing its short-term monetary policy to miss the targets in pursuit of the longer term goal.

Following the Bundesbank's target announcement stressing its continued adherence to monetary targeting after reunification and the lombard rate increase on February 1, long-term interest rates started falling for the first time since 1988. In hindsight, it is apparent that this was the beginning of a downward trend that continued until the bond market slump in early 1994. Although the highest inflation rates were still to come, at this point financial markets were apparently convinced that the Bundesbank would succeed in containing, if not reducing, inflation in the long run. By making it clear that it would not accommodate further price increases in the medium term, the Bundesbank bought itself flexibility for short-term easing without inviting misinterpretation. This link between transparency and enhanced flexibility, of course, depends upon the central bank's commitment to price stability being credible, but it emphasizes how even a credible central bank may gain through institutional design to increase transparency.

Until mid-August 1991, the Bundesbank left the discount and lombard rates unchanged, while the repo rate steadily edged up toward the lombard rate of 9 percent. CPI inflation in west Germany had still remained around 3 percent during the first half of 1991, while GDP growth remained vigorous. M3 growth, by contrast, was falling compared with its upward trend during late 1990, in part because of faster than expected portfolio shifts into longer term assets in east Germany.

These portfolio shifts, as well as the sharper than expected fall in the GDR's production potential, led the Bundesbank for the first time ever to change its monetary target on the occasion of its midyear review. The target for 1991 was lowered by 1 percent, to 3 to 5 percent. The fact that monetary targets are rarely reset is critical to any change being accepted without being perceived as a dodge by the central bank.

In this instance, the Bundesbank was able to invoke the implicit escape clause built into the semiannual target review. That formalized process, which required a clear explanation for any shift in targets, gave a framework for the Bundesbank to justify its adjustment. The discipline of the monetary targeting framework displayed the framework's disadvantages as well: that is, the difficulty of meeting short-run targets stemming from the instability of money demand and the inability to forecast changes in the monetary aggregate's relationship to goal variables.

As the repo rate approached the lombard rate again, the Bundesbank, on August 16, 1991, raised the lombard rate from 9 to 9.25 percent and the discount rate from 6.5 to 7.5 percent. The discount rate was raised to reduce the subsidy character of banks' rediscount facilities, which the Bundesbank had tolerated as long as the east German banks relied mostly on rediscount credit for the provision of their liquidity.

Despite the fact that GDP growth started to slacken during the second half of 1991, M3 growth accelerated. To some extent, the faster growth of M3 was a result of the by-then inverted yield curve, which led to strong growth of time deposits and prompted banks to counter the outflow from savings deposits by offering special savings schemes with attractive terms. This period was the first time that the yield curve had become inverted since the early 1980s and since the Bundesbank had been targeting M3. In this situation, the conflict arose for the Bundesbank that increases in interest rates were likely to foster M3 growth. This problem was all the more acute since banks' lending to the private sector was growing unabated despite the high interest rates, probably, to a large extent, because loan programs were subsidized by the federal government in connection with the restructuring of the east German economy and housing sector.

This conundrum, of the Bundesbank's instrument tending to work in the "wrong" direction, brought the underlying conflict of monetary targeting to the fore—the target must be critically evaluated constantly in relationship to the ultimate goal variable(s). However, if the target is cast aside regularly with reference to changes in that relationship or to special circumstances indicating a role for other intermediate variables, it ceases to serve as a target rather than solely as an indicator.

> Strictly defined, the use of a money growth target means that the central bank not only treats all unexpected fluctuations in money as informative in just this sense, but also, as a quantitative matter, changes its instrument variable in such a way as to restore money growth to the originally designated path. (Friedman and Kuttner 1996, p. 94)

The acceleration in late 1991 notwithstanding, M3 grew by 5.2 percent during 1991, close to the midpoint of the original target and just slightly above the revised target.

On December 20, 1991, the Bundesbank raised the lombard and discount rates by another 0.5 percent, to 9.75 percent and 8 percent, respectively, their highest levels since World War II (if the special lombard rates from the early 1970s are disregarded).

> In the light of the sharp monetary expansion, it was essential to prevent permanently higher inflation expectations from arising on account of the adopted wage and fiscal policy stance and the faster pace of inflation—expectations which would have become ever more difficult and costly to restrain. (Deutsche Bundesbank 1992a, p. 43)

The rhetoric invoked here by the Bundesbank is important to appreciate. Both government policies and union wage demands could be (and were) cited for their inflationary effects, that is, their pursuit of transfers beyond available resources. The Bundesbank may not have been able to override Chancellor Helmut Kohl's desired exchange rate of ostmarks for deutsche marks, or his "solidarity" transfers, but the Bundesbank Direktorium was comfortable in making it clear that the Kohl government and not the Bundesbank Direktorium should be held accountable for the inflationary pressures; the Bundesbank Direktorium took accountability for limiting the second-round effects of these pressures.

In addition to this division of accountability, the Bundesbank also clearly expressed some concern about the persistence of inflationary expectations and (if necessary) the cost of lowering them, thereby making clear its recognition of the substantial costs of disinflation even for a credible central bank. Finally, the Bundesbank's emphasis on the ultimate goal—medium-term price stability and inflation expectations—did not lead it to cite measures of private sector expectations directly—something, as we will see, many inflation targeters began doing at this time.

The December 20 increase in the lombard rate proved to be the last. During the first half of 1992, the repo rate slowly approached the lombard rate and peaked in August at 9.7 percent before starting to fall from late

August onward, as the Bundesbank started to ease monetary policy in response to the appreciation of the deutsche mark and emerging tensions in the European Monetary System; of course, the decision to ease also coincided with the rapid slowdown in German GDP growth. The monetary targets for 1992 and 1993 would not be met, but the challenge to German monetary policy from reunification was over.

> Thus in 1992, for example, when the money stock overshot the target by a large margin, the Bundesbank made it clear by the interest rate policy measures it adopted, that it took this sharp monetary expansion seriously. The fact that, for a number of reasons, it still failed in the end to meet the target . . . has therefore ultimately had little impact on the Bundesbank's credibility and its strategy. (Issing 1995b)

Monetary policy transparency was explicitly linked to flexibility during reunification, at least according to Bundesbank Chief Economist Otmar Issing, and that flexibility was exercised to minimize the real economic and political effects of maintaining long-term price stability.

Over the past five years or so, however, M3 has continued to prove itself a problematic intermediate target, even after reunification. The Bundesbank's own explanations for the sizable fluctuations in annualized M3 growth since 1992 (Chart 3, p. 34) suggest that demand for M3 behaves more and more like that for a financial asset rather than that for a medium of exchange. While the Bundesbank, in justifying deviations from the M3 targets, has begun giving greater prominence to reports on "extended money stock M3," a still broader aggregate that includes some recently growing forms of money market accounts, it has given no signs of readiness to switch target aggregates again (see Deutsche Bundesbank [1995b, July, p. 28]).

The Bundesbank has repeatedly described itself as "fortunate" because financial relationships have been more stable in Germany than in other major economies that have tried monetary aggregate targeting. It has attributed this successful experience to the self-described earlier deregulation of financial markets in Germany and the lack of inflationary or regulatory inducement for financial firms to pursue innovations. The targets continue as a structured framework by which the Bundesbank can regularly explain its monetary policy, even as the targets go unmet for periods of several years.[14]

In the December 1996 *Monthly Report*, the Bundesbank announced that it would set a target of 5 percent annualized growth in M3 in both 1997 and 1998. This is the first time since Germany adopted monetary targeting in 1975 that it has announced a multiyear monetary target. The explicit reason given for the multiyear target is to allow German monetary policy flexibility to respond to expected volatility in the currency markets in the run-up to European Monetary Union (EMU) in 1999, which would make these the last German monetary targets. Clearly, domestic price stability is balanced with other goals for the next two years and beyond, and flexibility, when viewed as publicly justifiable, is valued. Moreover, given the lags between movements in German monetary policy and their effects upon output and inflation, it is clear that the only variables that the Bundesbank can reasonably hope to influence significantly prior to EMU in 1999 are the evolving Exchange Rate Mechanism (ERM) parities.

The target range for M3 growth in 1997 will be 3.5 to 6.5 percent; the target range for 1998 will be announced at the end of 1997, apparently in response to the difference between actual M3 growth in 1997 and what is needed to achieve the 5 percent average. Bundesbank President Hans Tietmeyer indicated at the news conference announcing the new targets that the rate of annualized M3 growth in 1997-98 may be computed against the fourth quarter of 1995 rather than of 1996, because "comparison with the last quarter of 1996 can be a distortion." In 1996, M3 growth did exceed the Bundesbank's target range of 4 to 7 percent, with much of the difference being attributed to movements in narrow money in the last quarter as private households participated in the oversubscribed purchase of newly issued Deutsche Telecom stock. It is important to note as well, however, that 1996 inflation was at its lowest level in Germany since the adoption of monetary targets (1.4 percent growth in CPI)—and that the Bundesbank cut all three of its instrument interest rates to historical nominal lows—even as M3 growth exceeded the stated target.

The endgame nature of the current German monetary situation illustrates a point that is relevant for all inflation targeters with a fixed term for their targeting regime, a point that has not been relevant for Germany until now. When the end of the targeting regime is tied to a specific event—such as an election or a treaty commitment—it is not clear how much discipline the target imposes as that time approaches. A central bank could be less strict about target adherence in the early years of the period, making the claim that it will make up for temporary overshootings later. Yet, when this later time arrives, the commitment to return the targeted variable to a level required under the targeting regime will in effect predetermine the path of policy. The central bank is then unable to respond to economic events as they unfold unless it abandons the target.

In addition, the central bank may not be highly accountable for its monetary policy if the targeting regime is unlikely to be kept in place. If the central bank cannot be held accountable, then how can its target commitment be fully credible? This is not to suggest by any means that the Bundesbank will go "soft" on inflation in the run-up to EMU, but rather that it is best if target time horizons can be credibly extended before their expiration. As we will see in the case studies for both Canada and the United Kingdom, there was a need to reassure the public that targets would be maintained past election dates (and changes of political power).

KEY LESSONS FROM GERMANY'S EXPERIENCE

Germany's twenty years of experience with monetary targeting suggests two main lessons that are applicable to any targeting regime in which an inflation goal plays a prominent role. First, a targeting regime can be quite successful in restraining inflation even when the regime is flexible, allowing both significant overshootings and undershootings of the target in response to other short-run considerations. Indeed, German monetary targeting, although successful in keeping inflation low, must be seen as a significant departure from a rigid policy rule in which substantial target misses would not be tolerated.

Second, a key element of a successful targeting regime is a strong commitment to transparency. The target not only increases transparency by itself, but also serves as a vehicle to communicate often and clearly with the public and to promote an understanding of what the central bank is trying to achieve. We shall see that these key elements of a successful targeting regime—flexibility and transparency—have been present not only in the German case, but also in successful inflation-targeting regimes in other countries.

Economic Time Line: Germany

Chart 1

Annual and Unavoidable (Normative) Inflation

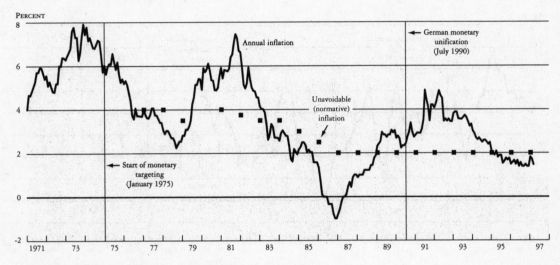

Sources: Deutsche Bundesbank; Bank for International Settlements.

Notes: "Unavoidable inflation" is the rate chosen by the Bundesbank for use in its quantity equation for monetary forecasts. In 1986, the Bundesbank renamed this rate "the rate of normative price increase."

Chart 2

Overnight and Long-Term Interest Rates

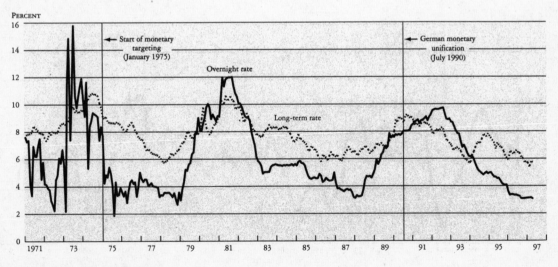

Source: Bank for International Settlements.

Chart 3

MONETARY GROWTH AND TARGETS

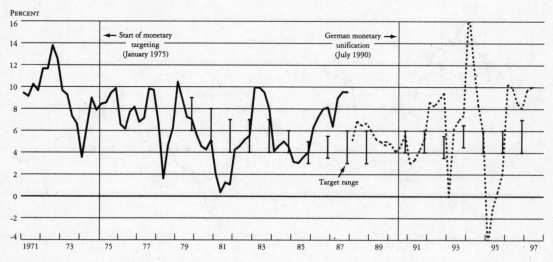

Sources: Deutsche Bundesbank; Bank for International Settlements.

Note: The shift to a dashed line indicates the change in the monetary aggregate targeted, from CBM (central bank money stock) to M3.

Chart 4

GDP GROWTH AND UNEMPLOYMENT

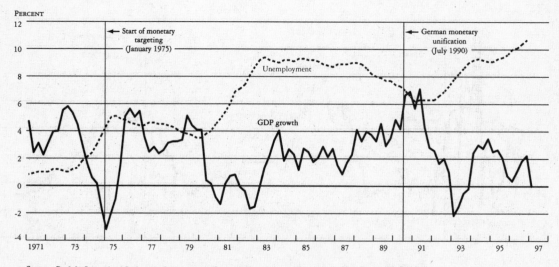

Sources: Bank for International Settlements; Organization for Economic Cooperation and Development, *Main Economic Indicators*.

Part IV.   New Zealand

New Zealand was the first country to adopt formal inflation targeting. In discussing its experience, we stress the following design choices and themes:

- Inflation targeting in New Zealand followed legislation that mandated a Policy Targets Agreement (PTA) between the elected government and the newly independent central bank, which resulted in a jointly decided numerical target for inflation.

- Inflation targeting was adopted only after a successful disinflation had largely taken place.

- Rather than using the headline consumer price index (CPI), the central bank uses a core-type price index to construct the inflation target variable; the variable excludes not only energy and commodity prices, but also, in particular, the effects of consumer interest rates as well as other prices on an ad hoc basis.

- The same entity that is accountable for achieving the inflation target, the Reserve Bank of New Zealand, also defines and measures the target variable when "significant" first-round impacts from terms-of-trade movements, government charges, and indirect taxes arise. The ultimate long-run target variable of CPI inflation, however, is compiled by a separate agency, Statistics New Zealand.

- Although New Zealand's inflation-targeting regime is the most rigid of the inflation-targeting regimes discussed in this study, it still allows for considerable flexibility: as in Germany, the central bank responds to developments in variables other than inflation, such as real output growth.

- Accountability of the central bank is a key feature of the inflation-targeting regime; the Governor of the central bank is subject to possible dismissal by the government if the target is breached.

- The inflation target is stated as a range, rather than as a point target—with the midpoint of this range above zero—again suggesting, as in the German case, that the long-term goal of price stability is defined as a measured inflation rate above zero.

- Strict adherence to the narrowness of the inflation target range and the one-year time horizon of the target has resulted in two related problems: 1) a control problem—that is, the difficulty in keeping inflation within very narrow target ranges—and 2) an instrument instability problem—that is, wider swings in the policy instruments, interest rates, and exchange rates than might have been desirable.

THE ADOPTION OF INFLATION TARGETS

The present framework for the conduct of monetary policy in New Zealand is explained by the Reserve Bank of New Zealand Act of 1989. The Act was introduced into Parliament by the government on May 4, 1989, was passed by Parliament on December 15, and took effect on February 1, 1990. It assigns to the Reserve Bank the statutory objective "to formulate and implement monetary policy directed to the economic objective of achieving and maintaining stability in the general level of prices" (Section 8).[1]

Although inflation targeting was the institutional means chosen to implement the Reserve Bank's commitment to price stability, the Act only put into the statute the need for a visible nominal anchor. Section 9 of the Act requires the Minister of Finance and the Governor of the Reserve Bank to negotiate and make public a Policy Targets Agreement, setting out "specific targets by which monetary policy performance, in relation to its statutory objective, can be assessed during the period of the Governor's term" (Lloyd 1992, p. 211). The first PTA, signed by the Minister of Finance and the Governor on March 2, 1990, specified numerical targets for inflation and the dates by which they had to be reached.

The passage of the Act and the establishment of numerical inflation targets have been the result of a slow process that started in July 1984. The then newly elected Labour Government embarked on a wide-ranging effort to reform the government's role in the New Zealand economy, tackling at the same time fiscal, monetary, structural, and external issues based on the view that these different aspects of economic policy were interrelated and thus had to be mutually coherent (for an overview of the reform measures, see Brash [1996b]). There was a general sense of crisis over New Zealand's economic policy at the time, based on concerns that the country's performance had been significantly lagging that of other members of the Organization for Economic Cooperation and Development (OECD) and that neither of the major party's old policies would work. As far as monetary performance went:

> New Zealand experienced double digit inflation for most of the period since the first oil shock. Cumulative inflation (on a CPI basis) between 1974 and 1988 (inclusive) was 480 per cent. A brief, but temporary, fall in inflation to below 5 per cent occurred in the early 1980s, but only as the result of a distortionary wage, price, dividend and interest rate freeze. Throughout the period, monetary policy faced multiple and varying objectives which were seldom clearly specified, and only rarely consistent with achievement of inflation reduction. As a result of this experience, inflation expectations were deeply entrenched in New Zealand society. (Nicholl and Archer 1992, p. 118)

Although the Reserve Bank stated that "a firm monetary policy is seen as an essential prerequisite for lower, more stable interest rates and inflation rates over the medium-term" (Reserve Bank of New Zealand 1985a, p. 451), at the start of the general reform movement there was no focused discussion of what exactly the objective(s) of monetary policy in the new economic environment should be. Initially, there was some indication of interest in intermediate targeting of monetary aggregates,[2] but this topic was never pursued and in recent years the Bank has stressed that no useful link exists between these aggregates and inflation.

At the time of the signing of the first PTA in March 1990, the Reserve Bank of New Zealand, backed by the Labour Government (which had been reelected in August 1987), had succeeded in bringing underlying inflation down from almost 17 percent at the beginning of 1985 to within the 5 percent range "although a number of one-off factors meant that only limited progress [on disinflation] was made" during 1989 (Reserve Bank of New Zealand 1990, p. 6). "The increase in GST [the goods and services tax in July 1989] pushed up the [headline] inflation rate and proved detrimental to inflation expectations. The GST damage was . . . compounded by the impact of strong commodity prices" (Reserve Bank of New Zealand 1990, p. 7). The decision to announce inflation targets occurred after most of the disinflation had already taken place. As we will also see in Canada, the announcement fortuitously was timed to cut off a rise in inflationary expectations and the original target was easily met.

THE OPERATIONAL FRAMEWORK

Most of the operational aspects of New Zealand's inflation-targeting framework are governed by the PTAs, since these agreements (and the targets they set) represent the only legal implementation of the Reserve Bank of New Zealand Act of 1989. The challenge for institutional designers in New Zealand was twofold: to determine, first, how far institutional change could take a very small natural-resource-based open economy to desired macroeconomic outcomes, and second, how to maintain appropriate public understanding of and support for counterinflationary policies after the initial reform impetus met with difficult developments. In general, New Zealand has opted to build in legal and formal means of introducing flexibility in its monetary framework. This choice of design opens the possibility of frequently announced changes in monetary policy variables and time horizons—with detailed legal accountability—albeit at some real cost in transparency to the general public. Within the exercise of this flexibility, the Reserve Bank still has had to balance the remaining constraints necessary for credibility with the realities of the world economy.

From the start, the eventual goal of price stability was defined in practice as achieving a rate of measured annual inflation of between 0 and 2 percent in the All Groups (that is, headline) CPI. The target was always intended to be a true range, with both the floor and ceiling to be taken seriously, but no special emphasis was placed on the midpoint. For example, in September 1991, policy was explicitly eased to avoid undershooting the range to encourage perceptions that the bands of the range were hard (Nicholl and Archer 1992, p. 124). Hitting the target remains an extremely ambitious goal because of the narrowness of the range and its centering so close to zero measured inflation—conditions that are costly to maintain in the face of external or commodity price shocks. The result has been that the actual inflation rate has remained near the top of the range for much of the time since the adoption of targets, with the public focus being on the 2 percent (ceiling) target rather than the 1 percent midpoint (the intended target).

Unlike Switzerland, a similarly small open economy that chose not to adopt a target range given the difficulties of controlling inflation exactly (especially so close to zero measured), the Reserve Bank clearly did not want to admit the likelihood of control problems, at least initially. As noted below, at the end of 1996 the band was widened, in part because the Reserve Bank recognized these difficulties. As a beginning for discussion, the Bank uses the CPI

> because it is the most widely known and the best understood index. . . . The above-zero rate of inflation specified reflects index number problems, the survey methodology, and the difficulty of adjusting for new goods or for improvements in quality. Effectively, a judgment has been made that 1 percent CPI inflation is consistent with stability in the general level of prices." (Nicholl and Archer 1992, p. 120)

The first PTA admitted that this headline CPI "is not an entirely suitable measure of [the prices of goods and services currently consumed by households] since it also incorporates prices and servicing costs of investment-related expenditures," most notably prices of existing dwellings, but the Agreement concluded that "the CPI will, for practical purposes, be the measure used in setting the targets" (Section 2).[3] The most difficult challenge for the Reserve Bank of New Zealand in communicating with the public about the target definition has arisen from the inclusion of interest rates in the headline CPI, as that is the main source of divergence from the target series. In the "Underlying Inflation" section of its August 1991 *Monetary Policy Statement*, the Bank stated that headline CPI "is the basic yardstick against which the Bank should be assessed" (Reserve Bank of New Zealand 1991, p. 17). It then stressed its emphasis in the recent past on controlling "underlying inflation" and continued:

> Unfortunately, because the nature of such shocks cannot be fully specified in advance, and because the impact of shocks can often not be measured precisely, it is not possible to specify a single, comprehensive definition of "underlying inflation." To some extent, interpretation of the impact and significance of the shocks is a matter of judgement, and hence requires clear explanations by the Bank to support any numerical estimates. (Reserve Bank of New Zealand 1991, p. 19)

In practice, therefore, the Bank has developed a measure of underlying inflation that it relies upon to exclude any of these shocks. (The first-round effect of interest rate changes on prices is automatically excluded in a series published by Statistics New Zealand, while other adjustments are left to the Bank.) Underlying inflation has been reported regularly alongside headline inflation by the New Zealand press as well as by the Reserve Bank, and there has been little confusion as the public has been educated over time (even as the two series diverged by as much as 2 percent in later years and have occasionally moved in opposite directions). This need to exclude items from the CPI series and then make sure the public understands why this action is legitimate is a challenge that all inflation targeters face. Even when a headline CPI series is used in inflation targeting, there is still a need to explain why the central bank should not respond to some deviations from the target (for example, identifiable temporary deviations from the trend such as hikes in the value-added tax).

It is useful to stress that this definition of underlying inflation has its advantages for New Zealand as the classic example of a small open economy. Without the terms-of-trade provision in the PTAs, for example, it is hard to see how monetary policy could limit variation in inflation to a meaningfully narrow range without causing severe disruption in real activity. Yet the judgmental aspect of this measure of inflation—that the Bank decides whether a given shock has a "significant" impact on the price level—is also potentially problematic. The most problematic aspect is that the Bank itself is in charge of defining the measure of inflation that determines whether the Bank has been successful in achieving the announced targets, an arrangement that undermines the seeming impartiality of the mechanism meant to hold the Bank accountable for achieving price stability.[4]

Another consequence of the Bank's efforts to communicate clearly and usefully about the distinction between headline and underlying inflation has to do with time horizons. Since the underlying inflation measure is not defined as a continuous series, but rather one with its composition changing at irregular intervals, this distinction adds to the potential confusion. It is worth pointing out, moreover, that the timing of the PTAs themselves—and therefore of the inflation target, however defined—is arbitrary, with the first interval lasting only six months and the latest lasting indefinitely. In light of the shift to open-ended targets, it is also worth noting that while the PTAs are not necessarily tied to the electoral cycle—set to expire with a given parliamentary majority—neither are they themselves statutorily insulated from such a cycle, and a new government could potentially renegotiate with the Bank as desired. The realization of this possibility, which occurred when the time horizon and range of the target were reset in December 1996, is discussed below.

A final aspect of timing is that neither the government nor the Bank has targeted the price level rather than the rate of inflation; the decision makers are letting bygones in earlier price-level rises be bygones. Either interpretation of price stability would have been consistent with the original Reserve Bank of New Zealand Act, as pointed out by Bryant (1996, p. 8). Since at the conclusion of the second PTA inflation had been within the 0 to 2 percent range for one year, both the third and fourth PTAs required the Bank merely to "formulate and implement monetary policy to ensure that price stability is maintained" indefinitely.

In practice, each of the PTAs has included a list of shocks in response to which the Bank is required to "generally react . . . in a manner which prevents general inflationary pressures emerging" (Section 3):[5] that is, the PTAs have escape clauses to accommodate first-round effects on prices but not to allow the passing on of these prices to a second round. These shocks include:

- a movement in interest rates that causes a significant divergence between the change in the CPI and the change in the CPI excluding the interest costs component. This clause of the third PTA replaced the earlier provision for a significant divergence between the CPI and a price index treating housing costs on an internationally comparable basis;

- significant changes in the terms of trade arising from an increase or decrease in either import or export prices;

- an increase or decrease in the rate of the goods and services tax (GST) or a significant change in other indirect taxes;

- a crisis such as a natural disaster or a major disease-induced fall in livestock numbers that is expected to have a significant impact on the price level; and

- a significant price-level impact arising from changes to government or local authority levies.

The Bank has consistently excluded from its measure of underlying inflation the effect of interest rate changes on mortgage and credit charges (relying on a series from Statistics New Zealand). It has also excluded the direct effects of any changes in indirect taxes and government and local authority levies when their impact on the CPI was judged to be significant (defined as an impact of at least 0.25 percent in any twelve-month period). Of course, this assessment of significance requires some decisions about modeling tax effects, and the Reserve Bank has chosen only to respond to those tax changes that were clearly driven by a policy decision.[6] The natural disaster escape clause has so far not been invoked. The terms-of-trade escape clause, however, has been applied in the discretionary manner allowed for in the PTAs. Twice, in 1990-91 and in 1994, oil price changes were excluded from the calculation of underlying inflation, while timber prices were excluded in 1993-94.

Caveats and escape clauses are meant to balance the Reserve Bank's inflation goal with other goals, particularly real economic goals in the face of supply shocks:

[A] detailed examination of what has been written about the caveats makes clear, the fundamental rationale for the caveats is that, in certain specified circumstances, the Reserve Bank should be paying attention to consequences for variables such as output and employment rather than concentrating single-mindedly on the inflation rate. (Bryant 1996, p. 24)

There was an absence of multiple stated objectives for the Reserve Bank, with only price stability listed in the Reserve Bank of New Zealand Act of 1989, and only supply shocks admitted as a potential reason for deviation. There were five reasons given for this single-minded focus: 1) monetary policy affects inflation only in the long run, 2) because monetary policy is only one instrument, it can deal with only one short-run goal at a time, 3) multiple objectives allow policy to change, which lowers credibility and raises inflationary expectations, 4) objectives partly undertaken by other government agencies if also pursued by the Reserve Bank could compromise the Bank's autonomy, and 5) multiple objectives reduce transparency and accountability since poor performance can then be attributed to the pursuit of the other objective (see Lloyd [1992] for a representative discussion). The explicit escape clauses were the only exception.

Whenever an inflation goal below current levels is to be achieved within a specified time horizon, this path of disinflation implies a judgment about the acceptable costs for achieving the lower inflation rate within the time frame. Because this choice affects the well-being of the public, it is inherently a political decision. That is why, in the New Zealand context, the choice was not left solely to the Reserve Bank. In this spirit, both the first and second PTAs envisaged a gradual transition to price stability over the three years following their signing and both called on the Bank to "publish a projected path for inflation for each of the years until price stability is achieved" (Section 5b).

The initial Policy Targets Agreement signed in March 1990 called for achievement of 0-2 percent inflation by December 1992 and maintenance of price stability thereafter. Partly as a result of a view that the output and employment costs of the speed of adjustment implicit in this time frame were too high, the new government elected in October 1990 deferred the target date by one year.[7] (Nicholl and Archer 1992, p. 120)

Clearly, the Reserve Bank of New Zealand under the 1989 Act was designed to operate as a very rule-based central bank. Notice the contrast between the PTA framework in New Zealand and that in Germany. Rather than seek an agreement with the government, the Bundesbank, when necessary, takes responsibility for setting the path of disinflation on its own, and then justifies that path directly to the general public.

In the time since the initial Policy Targets Agreement, the Reserve Bank has taken great pains to emphasize that the link between the real economy and monetary policy still exists in the short run, and that determining the speed of disinflation is the government's choice (and not the Bank's).[8] In the Reserve Bank's own words:

It should be emphasized, however, that the single price stability objective embodied in the Act does not mean that monetary policy is divorced from consideration of the real economy. At the technical level, the state of the real economy is an important component of any assessment of the strength of inflationary pressures. More importantly, inflation/real economy trade-offs may need to be made on occasion, particularly in the context of a decision about the pace of disinflation. . . . The main trade-offs are essentially political ones, and it is appropriate that they be made clearly at the political level. The framework allows trade-offs in areas such as the pace of disinflation, or the width of target inflation ranges, to be reflected in the PTA with the Governor. The override provision can also be used, if required, to reflect a policy trade-off.[9] (Lloyd 1992, p. 210)

Also, the Reserve Bank admits that there is still a short-run objective of financial stability, as all major central banks acknowledge.[10] "The Bank now has effective independence to implement monetary policy in pursuit of its statutory objective, without limitations on the technique except that the choices made must 'have regard to the efficiency and soundness of the financial system'" (Nicholl and Archer 1992, p. 119). The key point of this extended discussion of the true intent and functioning of the Bank's escape clauses, time horizons for targets, and beliefs about the relationship of monetary policy to goals other than price stability is to drive home the fact that even the Reserve Bank of New Zealand—the most extreme of all the inflation-targeting countries in its use of formal institutional constraints on monetary policy—is in operation not as constrained or as single-minded in its pursuit of price stability as some would have it.[11]

Since target adoption, the Reserve Bank has never assigned intermediate target status to any variable except the inflation target itself. It has consistently assigned low weight to developments in monetary and credit aggregates, reiterating that, since the beginning of the reforms in 1985, it is hard to establish any informative link between these aggregates and inflation. Over the past six years, in its public statements, it has paid the most attention to the trade-weighted exchange rate and the level and slope of the yield curve as part of an information-inclusive strategy:

> In building its forecasts of inflation pressures, the Bank has, over the last year or so, taken increasing account of the role of interest rates. Over the years, a better sense has emerged of the strength of the interest rate effect on demand, and hence inflation. . . . Short-term interest rate developments are now playing a greater role in the implementation of policy between formal forecast reviews, alongside the prominent role played by the exchange rate. (Reserve Bank of New Zealand 1995, p. 8)

This analysis of the yield curve emphasizes an interpretation of it as assessing monetary policy's stance or effect, rather than as a way of backing out an implicit inflation forecast. Inflation is chosen as the target just because it is the most practical nominal anchor available to New Zealand at this time—there is no reason a PTA could not be set up around another intermediate target.

> The judgment to date has been that a target specified in terms of the final inflation objective (suitably defined) is preferable to an intermediate monetary aggregate target, mainly because empirical work had not been able to identify any particular money aggregate which demonstrated a sufficiently close relationship with nominal income growth and inflation. (Lloyd 1992, p. 213)

In June 1987, well before the announced target adoption, the Bank started to conduct quarterly surveys of businesses' and households' expectations concerning a number of economic variables, among them inflation, and has regularly reported on developments in inflation expectations obtained from these as well as other surveys. Since then, the Reserve Bank has invested a great deal of effort and interest in the survey, which covers ten different macroeconomic variables and draws the majority of its respondents from the financial and business sectors. Questions and responses from the survey are published in the *Reserve Bank of New Zealand Bulletin* (discussed below). Price uncertainty, the Bank's greatest concern (rather than the point estimate of private sector inflation forecasts), is measured by the standard deviation of directly observed price-related expectations (Fischer and Orr 1994, p. 162).

All of these inflation-related data items and forecasts are assembled for public reading. Section 15 of the Reserve Bank of New Zealand Act of 1989 requires the Bank to produce, at least every six months, a policy statement that reviews the monetary policy of the previous six months and outlines how monetary policy is to be implemented over the next six months consistent with the Bank's stated inflation objective. These semiannual *Monetary Policy Statements* must be published and submitted to Parliament, and they may be discussed by a parliamentary select committee.

> They must review the implementation of monetary policy over the period since the last Statement, and detail the policies and means by which monetary policy will be directed towards price stability in the coming periods. The reasons for adopting the specified policies must also be given. The annual report provides a vehicle for accountability and monitoring of the Bank as a whole (not just in terms of monetary policy). This is also tabled in Parliament. The Governor and/or Deputy Governors are questioned by the Parliamentary Select Committee for Finance and Expenditure on both the Monetary Policy Statements and the annual reports. (Lloyd 1992, p. 214)

As noted, the Reserve Bank publishes an *Annual Report* and the *Reserve Bank of New Zealand Bulletin* with topical articles, reprinted speeches, and official statements. (Since the Reserve Bank of New Zealand Act of 1989, articles in the *Bulletin* have for the most part been attributed to their authors, encouraging more accountability and greater open discussion rather than presenting Bank policy as *deus ex machina*.) However, one major limitation remaining on the flow of information involves the collection and reporting of the various inflation series on a quarterly rather than monthly basis; it is not clear whether this reflects inherent data limitations in the New Zealand context or an intent to further smooth out noisy shifts in the inflation rate (and potential reactions by the markets) beyond those embodied in the "underlying" series and the various explanations.

Despite the tendency to classify the Reserve Bank's legal independence as akin to that of the Bundesbank or the Federal Reserve System, the Reserve Bank of New Zealand and its Governor actually face a much different situation. "This is not independence as the Bundesbank would understand it, since the target is to be set by the government and the Bank is responsible to the government for achieving it. The Bank is an agent, not a principal" (Easton 1994, p. 86). Put differently, while the two central banks share a similar goal, similarly defined, the Bundesbank's position is consistent with it being a trusted (and only informally or voluntarily accountable) institution. However, the structure of the Reserve Bank of New Zealand is consistent with its being an agency of the government held regularly to account. This is not a criticism of the Reserve Bank, either by observers or by the original legislators.

> The New Zealand reforms were motivated partly by orthodox economics and the desire to apply its precepts to government. However, they were also influenced by the political "New Right," which, on philosophical grounds, sought a smaller role for the public sector than perhaps could be justified from conventional economic theory alone. (Easton 1994, p. 78)

In addition, tighter constraints may have been necessary because of the past poor performance of New Zealand's monetary policy and the weaker public support for low inflation. The upshot for inflation targeting in New Zealand is that there is very little exercise of short-run discretion except as allowed by the caveats in the PTAs; moreover, that limited discretion must be accompanied by formal ex post communications with the government.

Accordingly, although these statements are made public in the *Monetary Policy Statements*, and in an active communication program beyond the *Statements* as pursued by the Bank, in New Zealand the burden of explanation falls less upon direct, transparent communications with the public than it does in countries where discretion is less constrained. This means that government support, rather than the power of the Reserve Bank's explanations to the public, is the source of flexibility.

NEW ZEALAND MONETARY POLICY
UNDER INFLATION TARGETING

This section summarizes the main events in New Zealand's monetary policy in the 1990s. It is based on the Bank's *Monetary Policy Statements* as well as on *OECD Economic Reports* and various newspaper reports.[12] Charts 1-4 (pp. 49-50), which track the paths of inflation, interest rates, the nominal effective exchange rate (henceforth the exchange rate), GDP growth, and unemployment in New Zealand both before and after inflation targeting, suggest that the period since New Zealand's adoption of inflation targets can be usefully divided into three episodes.

The first, from target adoption in March 1990 to March 1992, is characterized by inflation falling to within the 0 to 2 percent range, initially high interest rates (which later fell rapidly), a gradual decline in the exchange rate, negative GDP growth, and rising unemployment. During the second episode, from the second quarter of 1992 through the first quarter of 1994, inflation fluctuated within the upper half of the 0 to 2 percent range, interest rates continued to fall, the trend in the exchange rate was reversed, GDP growth rose sharply, and unemployment declined at a moderate pace. The third episode spans the last three years, when the Reserve Bank faced its greatest challenges since target adoption, and draws most of our attention. This situation since the second quarter of 1994 has been one of rising inflation and interest rates, continued appreciation of the exchange rate, sustained high GDP growth rates, and rapidly falling unemployment. During this episode, the inflation target was breached twice briefly, and was in fact reset as a result of an election.

The first episode begins with the initial Policy Targets Agreement, signed on March 2, 1990, stipulating that price stability, defined as annual inflation within the 0 to 2 percent range, was to be achieved by the year ending December 1992, and that each *Monetary Policy Statement* released by the Bank should contain a projected path for inflation over the following five years. The first *Monetary Policy Statement*, released in April 1990, specified that a 3 to 5 percent target range for inflation be reached by December 1990, a 1.5 to 3.5 percent range by December 1991, and a 0 to 2 percent range by December 1992 and thereafter. At this time, the Bank expected the economy to continue its gradual recovery during 1990 from the 1988 recession. The December 1989 figure for underlying inflation, excluding the effects of the 2.5 percent increase in the goods and services tax (GST) effective July 1, 1989, was 5.3 percent, and the Bank saw no need for changes in short-term interest rates at this point to achieve the first range in December 1990.

The two major surprises over the period through January 1991 covered by the second and third *Monetary Policy Statement*s were the oil price shock in the wake of the Iraqi invasion of Kuwait and the continued weakness of the New Zealand economy. In August 1990, the Bank tightened monetary policy somewhat in response to what it called the "fiscal slippage" evident in the budget released in July. In October, it announced that the target range for December 1990 should apply to CPI inflation excluding oil prices. The oil price adjustments were then used as a pedagogic occasion for the Bank to specify that in the future, targets would apply to underlying inflation. As it turned out, inflation including oil prices over the year to December 1990 was 4.9 percent—inside the original target range—but by then the target ranges had been changed.

Following its victory by a large margin in the general election on October 29, 1990, the new majority National (right) Government signed a new PTA with the Bank on December 19, extending the disinflation process by one year. As noted above, this extension was due to the elected government's belief that rapid disinflation had already proved too costly in real terms. This view was widely held, and the domestic financial sector was extremely outspoken in characterizing the 0 to 2 percent inflation target range as a dangerous "obsession."[13] Nevertheless, before the election both the Labour and the National Parties (the two main parties in the then-majoritarian, rather than proportional representation, parliamentary system) supported maintaining the inflation targets at their original level.[14] These developments illustrate the many ways in which an inflation target can be adapted without a change in the primary target definition, with the time horizon being a critical determinant (as explained above) of how tightly the target constrains policy.

The February 1991 *Monetary Policy Statement* specified the inflation target range at 2.5 to 4.5 percent by December 1991, 1.5 to 3.5 percent by December 1992, and 0 to 2 percent by December 1993 as the new path toward price stability. Already in mid-November 1990, the Bank started to allow the ninety-day bank bill rate to fall substantially in response to lower than expected inflationary pressure due to only modest effects of the oil price increases, sluggish domestic growth, and what was seen as the new government's support of the goal of price stability. (The bill rate is indicative of the stance of the Reserve Bank's monetary policy, but unlike a true policy instrument it is not directly controlled by the Bank.[15]) By mid-January 1991, the bill rate had fallen to under 11.5 percent from 14.6 percent in August 1990.

By August 1991, the Bank had expressed its surprise at the speed at which inflation was falling. Growth in wage settlements was low, unit labor costs were essentially unchanged, the exchange rate was stable, and import prices were flat, reflecting the recession in a number of major economies. Whereas in its February 1991 *Monetary Policy Statement* the Bank had expected headline inflation to be slightly above the midpoint of the 2.5 to 4.5 percent range by the next December, in the quarter to June it was already down to 2.8 percent, and the Bank's forecast for the year up to December 1991 was 2 percent. Likewise, underlying inflation (with mortgage interest rates, oil prices, and indirect taxes and government charges removed) was down to 2.6 percent by June and was expected to fall below 2.5 percent by the end of the year. The Bank stated that "this outcome will reflect the firm policy stance maintained throughout

[1990], and some imprecision in the process of controlling inflation" (Reserve Bank of New Zealand 1991, p. 43).

By late September, the Bank started to ease monetary policy sharply "when it became clear that, in the absence of this action, underlying inflation for 1992 was likely to fall below the 1.5 to 3.5% indicative range" (Reserve Bank of New Zealand 1992a, pp. 5-6). In order to maintain the floor on the range as part of the explicit commitment (without seeming to be motivated by any apparent fears of deflation), the Reserve Bank allowed the ninety-day bank bill rate to fall to 8.8 percent over the next three months and the exchange rate to depreciate sharply. Already by October, the New Zealand dollar was at its lowest level against the currencies of its trading partners in five years, but the Bank and the Prime Minister explained to the public that the depreciation would not imperil the achievement of future inflation targets because of the forecast and the nature of the depreciation.[16] In December 1991, headline and underlying inflation were down to 1 percent and 1.7 percent, respectively, roughly 1 percent below the forecasts from August. "The contraction in the domestic economy (which itself was more marked than anticipated) impacted on inflationary pressures to a greater extent than had been expected" (Reserve Bank of New Zealand 1992a, p. 10). Also, world prices had been lower and the exchange rate held firm for longer than had been expected. Mostly as a result of the exchange rate depreciation, the Bank expected underlying inflation to peak at around 3 percent by early 1993 and then to fall back to 1.2 percent by the end of that year.

The June 1992 *Monetary Policy Statement* heralds the beginning of the second episode, stating that "the Bank is now focusing on ensuring that price stability is consolidated, rather than on still trying to achieve significant reductions in inflation" (Reserve Bank of New Zealand 1992b, p. 13). In the year from March 1991 to March 1992, headline and underlying inflation had fallen to 0.8 percent and 1.3 percent, respectively. The domestic economy had entered the recovery in recent months and the Bank therefore saw that its task now was to maintain price stability in an environment of moderate growth. The continued favorable outlook for inflation and the reduction in inflation expectations, as documented by the Bank's surveys, had allowed the Bank to accommodate some further easing, with the ninety-day bank bill rate falling to 6.6 percent. The Bank's forecasts for underlying inflation for the end of 1992 and for 1993 were now at 2 percent and 1 percent, respectively, reflecting primarily downward revisions in expected unit labor costs and import prices. The turning point in the exchange rate, in January 1993, was foreshadowed by the Bank's assessment that "over the longer run . . . if the inflation rates of our trading partners . . . remain higher than that in New Zealand, some appreciation of the nominal exchange rate would be entirely consistent with the maintenance of price stability" (Reserve Bank of New Zealand 1992b, p. 35).[17]

Some unrest in the currency market following the release of the December 1992 *Monetary Policy Statement* prompted a moderate tightening action by the Bank, reflected in a rise in the ninety-day bank bill rate from 6.4 percent to 7.8 percent. Apart from this brief incident, the period from mid-1992 until the end of 1993 is best described by the absence of any challenges to monetary policy. The domestic economy continued its recovery without any notable inflationary pressures appearing. The ninety-day bank bill rate fell below 5 percent in December 1993. Private sector inflation expectations remained by and large unchanged, and the Bank's inflation forecasts one and two years ahead remained comfortably inside the 0 to 2 percent range. Donald Brash had been reappointed Governor of the Reserve Bank on December 16, 1992, reflecting the Reserve Bank's perceived strength, while the National Party barely survived the next election, holding on to a one-seat majority in Parliament. At the end of 1992, a new PTA was signed between the Bank and the National Party, specifying that the Reserve Bank must maintain underlying CPI within the already achieved 0 to 2 percent range.

As the most recent period in New Zealand monetary policy began, continuing domestic expansion and appreciation of the exchange rate shifted the risks of future inflation from external to domestic sources. With hindsight, it is clear that inflationary pressures started to develop in early 1994. In December 1993, the Bank noticed indications that the recovery might be stronger than anticipated, but still considered it "premature" to tighten policy. Its forecast of underlying inflation by the end of 1994 and 1995 was at 0.8 percent and 1.8 percent, respectively. One recurring topic covered in the *Monetary Policy Statements* during the period since early 1994 is the Bank's uncertainty about the level of growth that the New Zealand economy could sustain without creating inflation. The structural reforms initiated since 1985, primarily the liberalization and opening of markets to international competition and institutional changes in the wage-setting process, were presumed to have made it more difficult for price and wage inflation to develop. Combined with an assumed increase in the credibility of the monetary policy framework, the reforms could have allowed higher growth rates to be sustained without igniting inflation than was the case during previous business cycles. Forecasting the actual size of these effects proved to be difficult.

In line with the seeming thrust of these effects, the average ninety-day bank bill rate dropped from 5.5 percent in the December 1993 quarter to 4.9 percent in the March 1994 quarter, even as it became clear that GDP had grown 5 percent during 1993. Over the second quarter of 1994, monetary policy started to respond to the unexpected strength of the economy, and the average ninety-day bank bill rate rose to 6.2 percent through June. GDP was growing at a rate of 6 percent per year with all sectors displaying rapid expansion, most notably the construction sector. Capacity utilization had been on an upward path since late 1991, despite strong investment over the preceding years, and employment had grown at an annual rate of 4 percent since the beginning of the year. By midyear 1994, private sector economists began to worry that a breach of the target range by headline CPI might give rise to increasing inflation expectations by the public, even if underlying CPI inflation remained on target. From June to December, the bill rate rose from 5.5 percent to 9.5 percent. As a result, the yield curve turned negatively sloped again. The exchange rate had appreciated by 4.5 percent over 1994.

At this point, the Bank's assessment was "that the economic upturn may have peaked, and that growth may begin to moderate over the coming year" (Reserve Bank of New Zealand 1995). However, its forecast of underly-

ing inflation over the next two years came very close to the 2 percent upper bound, with underlying inflation expected to stay around 1.8 percent over all of 1995 and headline inflation peaking at 4.2 percent in the second quarter of 1995, mainly as a consequence of rising mortgage rates. A number of private forecasts disagreed with the Bank's, predicting a target breach in mid-1995. Finance Minister William Birch found it necessary to respond to press questions about whether Governor Brash would in fact be dismissed if the target were breached. His response, unsurprisingly, was that the Reserve Bank's forecasts did not offer any grounds for believing that the target would be breached.[18]

The Bank's forecast for both GDP growth and inflation in 1995 proved to have been too low. In May, the Reserve Bank revised its forecast to predict that underlying inflation would exceed the 2 percent target ceiling in the second quarter of 1995. But "Mr. Brash said the Bank remained confident the underlying inflation rate would fall back during the third quarter of this year, and therefore planned to take no action on a 'temporary' breach" (Tait 1995). Governor Brash made it clear that the overshooting would not be reversed so long as there was no trend behind it, but that he did not anticipate expectations to respond unduly to a "temporary" deviation. This episode illustrates, however, that the government's view of the inflation-targeting framework in New Zealand consciously denies the framework's consistency with an "averaging" approach (why else would the government make an immediate request for the explanation of a 0.2 percent target breach?). This rigidity, given the inevitability of target breaches due to policy uncertainty, especially for a narrow target, is problematic.

Although during the second and third quarters of 1995 there were some signs of a slowdown in economic activity, by the end of the year the outlook had become more mixed, with some indication that GDP growth would pick up again, leading the Bank to forecast GDP growth of 1.5 percent in the year to March 1996 and 3 percent in the year to March 1997. More important, from the Bank's point of view, measured underlying inflation did in fact rise above the 0 to 2 percent range to peak at 2.2 percent in the second quarter, with headline inflation rising to 4.6 percent (although both remained below the outer bounds of private sector forecasts).

Thereafter, headline inflation fell rapidly, as the rise in mortgage rates stemming from the monetary tightening during 1994 stopped having an effect on the CPI calculation (an effect that was excluded from the definition of underlying inflation). Underlying inflation, by contrast, fell to only 2 percent in the year to September 1995, and although in June 1994 the Bank still had expected underlying inflation to return to 1.2 percent by June 1996, its December 1995 forecast for the year to September 1996 was 1.7 percent. A major factor behind the increase in underlying inflation was the persistent construction boom, particularly in the Auckland area, in which construction costs increased by 11.8 percent over the year to March 1995.

This concentration of inflationary pressures in the nontraded sector made the Bank's monetary policy less effective in slowing prices than past experience indicated because the exchange rate channel of monetary transmission would have little impact on this sector of the economy. As a result, keeping inflation within the tight target range required a sharp rise in nominal interest rates (to more than 9 percent) and a sharp appreciation of the New Zealand dollar. The required movements of interest and exchange rates can be characterized as the result of a very small economy running an independent monetary policy when its economic cycle is out of phase with the major world economies. In addition, these movements can be a potential source of instrument instability, with resulting economic dislocations.[19] Nevertheless, the key accomplishment that New Zealand observers saw was that the country had, for the first time in decades, been through a business cycle upswing of strong growth without a balance-of-payments or inflation crisis at the end of it.

Governor Brash did take "full responsibility" for the Bank's not having acted sooner to stem inflationary pressures, thereby allowing the target to be breached. Citing the "temporary" nature of the breach, however, he said that he would not resign, and Finance Minister Birch backed him (Hall 1995). Clearly, the dismissal of the Reserve Bank Governor for breach of the target is not automatic, either in design or in practice. Rather, dismissal is left to the judgment of the Board and the Finance Minister. However, from the point of view of an "optimal central banking contract"—as many have characterized the New Zealand framework—Governor Brash was not penalized for exceeding the specific number set in the contract.

By October 1995, inflation had subsided, but Governor Brash was sufficiently chastened by the experience to suggest that he would rather see the Bank have an inflation target in which the goal was in the center of the range, given the difficulties of forecasting. "You don't have any room for being wrong at a rate of 1.8 to 1.9 percent" (Montagnon 1995). The gap between how finely it is possible for the Reserve Bank to control inflation and the narrow range to which the Reserve Bank was committed became the main theme for the next year. The target breach illustrated the potential for instrument instability, in which the policy instruments need to undergo wide swings in order to achieve inflation targets narrower than a small economy's monetary policy can consistently provide.

Since the inflation target goal required of the Bank results from the PTA with the elected government—and the response (that is, whether or not to dismiss the Governor) to target breaches also depends upon the government's support—monetary policy became a highly visible political issue in the run-up to the October 1996 elections. The primary debate centered on whether the target range should be widened, although some minor parties considered altering the goal of monetary policy from 1 percent measured inflation. In December 1995, the Reserve Bank tightened policy again. Most observers characterized this as a reaction to tax cuts announced by the National Party meant to take effect right before the elections nine months later; Finance Minister Birch publicly denied this interpretation, stating that the size and nature of the tax cuts had been discussed with the Reserve Bank before being put through Parliament (Birch 1996). In any event, the issue in the popular mind had moved from one of low inflation to one of high real interest rates. By February 1996, Governor Brash felt it necessary to open a speech to the Auckland Manufacturers' Association with the following remarks:

Over recent weeks there have been a number of media reports of people calling for the abolition of the Reserve Bank, or the repeal of the Reserve Bank Act, with the claim that the Bank is an anachronism in New Zealand's free-market economy, that its operations result in New Zealanders having to pay interest rates which are among the highest in the world in real terms, and that these interest rates are pushing up the exchange rate to the huge detriment of exporters and those competing with imports. There are variations around this theme, depending upon who is mounting the case, but I think that I accurately reflect the general case. (Brash 1996b)

While Governor Brash's policies had contained trend inflation sufficiently to justify the government's support, the differential effects of tight money on traded and non-traded goods exacerbated the public political fallout of having to maintain high interest rates to achieve the required tight control. Simply meeting the contract was not enough when the contract itself came under fire, and even though rewriting the contract was the politicians' responsibility and not the Bank's, the Bank began to suffer the consequences.

On April 19, 1996, the Board of the Reserve Bank sent a letter to Finance Minister Birch. It had become clear that the target ceiling would be breached again by mid-year, that headline inflation would rise while underlying inflation would only temporarily rise again, and that the issue of dismissing the Governor would have to be dealt with once more, even though again no one felt that policy was too loose or that inflation expectations were slipping. However, the fact that the Reserve Bank was running into a control problem for the second time in a year pointed out the difficulties of the third PTA. The Board's letter supported Governor Brash's performance—carefully basing the argument mostly on the trend of underlying inflation—and recommended that he continue in his position.

In May, however, the New Zealand First Party—a populist party likely to become a coalition member for the first time in the November elections once multimember proportional representation had replaced majoritarian elections[20]—advocated the addition of unemployment and growth goals for monetary policy. Between the upcoming

likelihood of an inflation blip and the political uncertainty being tied to monetary policy, long-term bond yields rose, and the spread between ten-year bond rates in New Zealand and the United States reached 200 basis points, the highest level since 1992. The Labour Party made a proposal of its own to widen the band to -1 to 3 percent inflation.

In June 1996, the Reserve Bank reported that underlying inflation did in fact breach the target ceiling of 2 percent in the first quarter, and it forecast that underlying inflation would reach 2.6 percent in the third quarter. When historically high real interest rates appeared to be insufficient to maintain inflation within the target range consistently, the feasibility of the target range was questioned more widely. Private sector economists began to join the opposition parties in advocating a widening of the target range, predicting that inflation would remain above 2 percent through March 1997. Of course, the Reserve Bank, among others, feared that a widening of the range might be interpreted as a weakening of anti-inflationary resolve and would have harmful effects on credibility and inflation expectations; as noted above, however, even Governor Brash had come to realize that the control problems of a 0 to 2 percent target range were too great for monetary policy in the New Zealand economy.

Dr. Brash acknowledged that it would be tempting to say that the 0 to 2 percent target range was both too low and too narrow. But . . . "I don't think it is self-evident at all that a wider target would help the real economy," Dr. Brash said. "On the contrary there are some real risks in doing that." The dangers were that widening the range would itself raise inflationary expectations, and that the Reserve bank itself would be slower to react to inflationary pressures. The width of the target band is only one of the features of the present monetary policy framework to be questioned of late. (Fallow 1996)

Only successful targeters of long standing, like Germany and Switzerland, appeared to be able to explain frequent target range misses without changing their ranges. Given the starting premises of the Reserve Bank of New Zealand Act of 1989 and its inflation-targeting framework, the need to control inflation tightly every quarter (or to formally justify the Governor's retaining his position) when New Zealand's monetary policy could only do so much, created pressure for a more activist monetary policy than was ever originally intended. In particular, the interaction between domestic interest rates oriented toward fighting inflation and the exchange rate harmed the competitiveness of export sectors of the economy.

On October 12, 1996, New Zealand held its first mixed-member proportional representation elections for national Parliament; the outcome was (as expected) indecisive, with no one party getting more than 50 percent of the vote. The New Zealand First Party clearly held the balance in making a coalition, negotiating with both the Labour and National Parties. On October 18, National Party (and caretaker) Finance Minister Birch publicly indicated that the inflation target (its width, its average level) was on the table in negotiations with the New Zealand First Party. The October 16 data release showed underlying inflation remaining above target at 2.3 percent (headline inflation was 2.4 percent), but below some private forecasts that were as high as 2.7 percent. In the words of one New Zealand business columnist watching the negotiations, "the message: [despite being generally successful,] present Reserve Bank inflation targets are not credible. They could be changed at any time, depending on the whims of whoever wants most to drive about in a ministerial LTD. We are back to politicized monetary policy" (Coote 1996).

Meanwhile, the Bank found itself on the horns of its ongoing dilemma. The New Zealand dollar had risen to an eight-year high against the yen and the U.S. dollar as capital flowed back into New Zealand after the election. The Bank again was confronted with difficult choices. Despite the above-target contemporaneous inflation rate and the need to rein in inflationary pressures on the non-traded goods side—and because of the medium-term trend of underlying inflation and the highly unfavorable circumstances for the traded goods sector—there was good reason not to raise interest rates further. "Unfortunately, in order to keep overall monetary conditions consistent with maintaining price stability, it appears we have to accept rather less interest rate pressure than might be ideal, and rather more exchange pressure than might be ideal," stated the Bank on October 24 (Hall 1996a). In other words, the

Bank was admitting that its control problem of hitting the required narrow target range forced it into short-run policy trade-offs that it did not want, given the political constraints of the tight target.

Finally, on December 10, a parliamentary coalition between the National and New Zealand First Parties was agreed to for a three-year term. Their first substantive announcement was that the inflation target would be modified. The new Policy Targets Agreement was signed by the National Party's Finance Minister Birch and Governor Brash on December 10. The shift effectively underlines the inescapably political nature of a central bank's accountability under any democratic system: that is, that the goal by which the monetary framework is evaluated, and in the New Zealand case the exercise of the option to dismiss the Governor for not attaining the goal, reflect the current elected officials' preferences.

On December 18, Governor Brash characterized the widening of the inflation target from 0 to 2 percent to 0 to 3 percent as a modest change: "We previously aimed at inflation of 1 per cent. It is now 1.5 per cent" (Hall 1996b). While Governor Brash admitted that this would allow some easing, he stated that it was already justified by inflation forecasts: "to the extent that increased inflationary expectations lead to higher prices, higher wage settlements and so on, the new inflation target gives much less scope for an easing . . . than might perhaps be assumed" (Tait 1996). To the extent possible, the Reserve Bank was intent on limiting any damage to its credibility.

In an address given a month later (Brash 1997), Governor Brash summarized the meaning of the new PTA, including the amended inflation target. He emphasized that "price stability remains the single objective of monetary policy and constitutes the best way in which the Reserve Bank can contribute to New Zealand's economic development." He noted that the current state of knowledge in monetary economics left unresolved the debate between those who advocate a "low, positive inflation" and those who argue for zero inflation. The Governor continued,

"it is at this stage quite inappropriate to be dogmatic, and in my own view a target which involves doing our utmost to keep measured inflation between

0 and 3 percent is certainly consistent with the intention of the legislation within which monetary policy is operated. . . . Indeed, irrespective of where the mid-point of the target range should be, there may be some advantage in having a slightly wider inflation target than the original 0 to 2 percent target. A number of observers have suggested that a target with a width of only 2 percentage points requires an excessive degree of activism on the part of the central bank. . . . The tension is between, on the one hand, choosing a target range which effectively anchors inflation expectations at a low level but which is so narrow that it provokes excessive policy activism and risks loss of credibility by being frequently exceeded; and on the other, a target range which does a less effective job of anchoring inflation expectations, but which requires less policy activism and protects credibility by being rarely breached. (Brash 1997)

KEY LESSONS FROM NEW ZEALAND'S EXPERIENCE

After close to seven years of inflation targeting, the Reserve Bank of New Zealand's experience provides several important lessons. First, it suggests that the challenge of bringing down trend inflation and maintaining low inflation expectations is relatively easy compared with that of tightly controlling the course of inflation within a narrow range, especially for a small open economy. Furthermore, New Zealand's experience indicates that strict adherence to a narrow inflation target range can lead to movements in policy instruments that may be greater than the central bank would like and open the potential for instrument instability should the pressures from these movements become too great.

In addition, the Reserve Bank has found that excessive restrictions on the exercise of its discretion and the manner of its explanation of policy—even if in the name of accountability—can create unnecessary instances in which credibility could be damaged even when underlying trend inflation is contained. This is due not only to inflexibility, but also to the Bank's focus on direct, formal accountability to the government rather than a broader accountability to the general public through transparency.

These lessons about the operation of targeting frameworks do not negate the fact that inflation targeting in New Zealand has been highly successful: this country, which was prone to high and volatile inflation before the inflation-targeting regime was implemented, has emerged from the experience as a low-inflation country with high rates of economic growth.

Economic Time Line: New Zealand

Chart 1

Underlying Inflation, Headline Inflation, and Targets

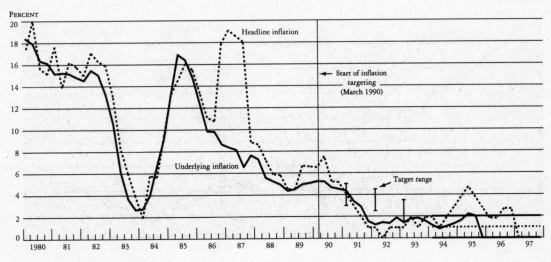

Source: Reserve Bank of New Zealand.

Note: The I-shaped bars indicate the target range for inflation in effect before the adoption of an ongoing target range of 0 to 2 percent in March 1994; a dashed horizontal line marks the midpoint of the ongoing target range.

Chart 2

Bank Bill and Long-Term Interest Rates

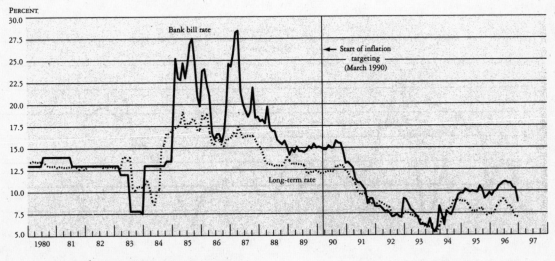

Source: International Monetary Fund, *International Financial Statistics.*

Chart 3

NOMINAL EFFECTIVE EXCHANGE RATE

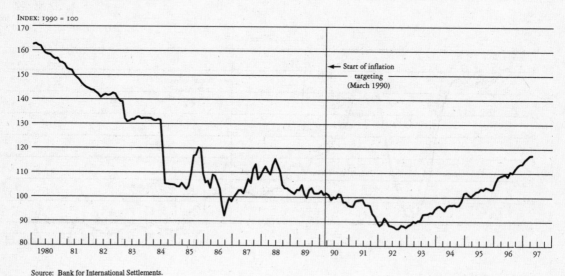

Source: Bank for International Settlements.

Chart 4

GDP GROWTH AND UNEMPLOYMENT

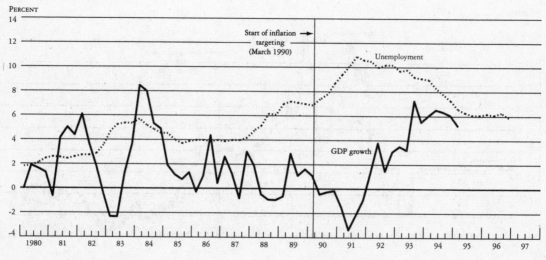

Source: Reserve Bank of New Zealand.

Part V.   Canada

anada adopted inflation targeting in 1991, one year after New Zealand. In examining its experience, we stress the following themes:

- Inflation targeting in Canada was not the result of legislation. However, as in New Zealand, the inflation target in Canada is jointly determined and announced by both the government and the central bank.

- As in New Zealand, inflation targeting was adopted after substantial disinflationary pressures were already evident.

- In Canada, there is a clear-cut separation between the entity that measures the inflation variable to be targeted (Statistics Canada) and the entity that is accountable for achieving the inflation target and assessing past performance (the Bank of Canada).

- The consumer price index (CPI) inflation rate has been chosen as the primary target variable because of its "headline" quality, although a core inflation rate that excludes energy and food prices and the effects of indirect taxes is also used and reported in assessing whether the trend inflation rate is on track for the medium term.

- The Canadian inflation-targeting regime is quite flexible in practice, as are all the regimes we study, with real output growth and fluctuations a consideration in the conduct of monetary policy. Indeed, in Canada, the inflation target is viewed as a way to help dampen cyclical fluctuations in economic activity.

- In Canada, as in New Zealand and even Germany, the chosen rate of convergence of the medium-term inflation goal to the long-term goal has been quite gradual.

- The Canadian inflation target is stated as a range rather than a point target, often with greater emphasis placed on the bands than on the midpoint.

- The midpoint of the inflation target range, 2 percent, is above zero, as in all the cases we examine here.

- Although accountability is a central feature of the inflation-targeting regime in Canada, the central bank is more accountable to the public in general than to the government directly.

- A key and increasingly important feature of Canada's inflation-targeting regime is a strong commitment to transparency and the communication of monetary policy strategy to the public.

- As an adjunct to implementing the inflation-targeting regime, the central bank makes use of a monetary conditions index (MCI), a weighted average of the exchange rate and the short-term interest rate, as a short-run operating target.

THE ADOPTION OF INFLATION TARGETS

The adoption of inflation targeting in Canada on February 26, 1991, followed a three-year campaign by the Bank of Canada to promote price stability as the long-term objective of monetary policy. This campaign, beginning with then Governor John Crow's Hanson Lecture at the University of Alberta in January 1988, "The Work of Canadian Monetary Policy" (Crow 1988), had spelled out the reasons for the Bank of Canada's disinflationary policy of the late 1980s and early 1990s. The campaign had not, however, spelled out the practical policy implications of what price stability meant in terms of either inflation levels or the time frame for reaching that goal (Thiessen 1995d; Freedman 1994a, 1995).

On February 26, 1991, formal targets through the end of 1995 "for reducing inflation and establishing price stability in Canada" were announced. The announcement was a joint statement by the Minister of Finance, Michael

Wilson, of the ruling Conservative Party, and the Governor of the Bank of Canada, John Crow. Publicity was maximized by the timing of the announcement, which occurred on the day of the Canadian government's release of its budget and underscored the government's support of the Bank's commitment to the goal of price stability. The following month, the Bank released its *Annual Report, 1990*, which featured remarks by Governor Crow on the appropriateness of price stability as a goal for monetary policy and an article entitled "The Benefits of Price Stability" (Bank of Canada 1991a). The initiation of the new monetary policy commitment to inflation targeting had been carefully planned to attract public attention and to begin building public support.

Yet there had been no advance notice to the public of the policy shift to inflation targeting by senior Bank of Canada officials. Even in the same *Annual Report, 1990*, a one-paragraph mention of the announcement of inflation targets was tacked on the end of Governor Crow's annual statement, with no mention of the adoption earlier in the piece. Nor was there an obvious crisis prompting an abrupt shift in policy (such as a devaluation and exit from a fixed exchange rate system or the sudden breakdown of a declared intermediate target relationship). Governor Crow had been appointed to his position four years earlier, and the Conservative Government had been reelected in late 1988, so a change in policymakers also did not explain the shift in policy.

Before the announcement of specific inflation targets, the Bank's repeated declaration of the price stability goal by itself appeared to have made little headway against the "momentum" in inflation expectations that had built up (Thiessen 1991; Freedman 1994a). In fact, in the "Background Note" released at the time of the adoption of the targets, mention is made of the "unduly pessimistic" outlook for inflation in a number of quarters (Bank of Canada 1991c, p. 11). Inflation targets were the tactic adopted to reduce sticky expectations and to bring the stated goal of Canadian monetary policy to fruition.

February 1991, it turns out, was seen by the Bank of Canada as a useful opportunity to formalize its commitment to price stability. On the positive side, year-over-year CPI inflation had just dropped to 4.2 percent in the fourth quarter of 1990 (versus a high of 5.5 percent in early 1989), and "the pressures from excess demand that were pushing up prices from 1987 through 1989 finally eased during 1990" (Thiessen 1991), with economic growth at its cyclical trough. Because the Canadian economy had slowed—and, although not realized at the time, had entered a deep recession in 1990—underlying disinflationary pressures were already becoming apparent at the time the targets were introduced.

More important, on the negative side, large risk premiums were being built into long-term Canadian interest rates because of rapidly growing government and external debt, political uncertainty, and credibility problems for monetary policy following two decades of inflation. Furthermore, a new goods and services tax (GST)—an indirect tax similar to a value-added tax (VAT)—was to take effect at the start of 1991 with an expected effect on the headline total CPI of 1.25 percent, and there were fears of further oil price increases as well. A failure to keep the first-round effects of the indirect tax increase from initiating a new wage-price spiral would only confirm the public's high inflation expectations.

The current Governor of the Bank of Canada, Gordon Thiessen, characterized February 1991 as period of public uncertainty, despite the prior declarations of the price stability goal (Thiessen 1991, 1995d). Deputy Governor Charles Freedman (1994a) also stated that one of the Bank of Canada's primary short-run concerns was to prevent an upward spiral in inflation expectations in the face of these shocks. The Bank went further and seized the opportunity to distinguish between the temporary shocks and the intended path of inflation as an instructional precedent for its targeting framework. As the initial announcement explained: "These targets are designed to provide a clear indication of the downward path for inflation over the medium term" (Bank of Canada 1991b). To underscore this intention, the Bank referred to them as "inflation-reduction targets," until the target range stopped dropping in 1995. Of course, the targets chosen were thought to be realistically attainable, the logic being that if declarations of the price stability goal were not enough, failure to achieve the promised amount of progress toward that goal would certainly be detrimental (Freedman 1995).

The Bank set the first target for twenty-two months after the announcement of target adoption for the stated reason that six-to-eight-quarter lags in the effect of monetary policy made any earlier target infeasible. Canada possibly went through a period of significant inflation uncertainty as a result, and inflation *undershot* the target range until early 1993. The targets did not appear believable to the public until later (Laubach and Posen 1997b). In contrast, New Zealand's and the United Kingdom's target ranges took effect immediately upon adoption, and these countries experienced little problem with target misses until their recent cyclical upswings.

The Bank of Canada's intellectual basis for its inflation-targeting approach—and for its goal of price stability, rather than just low inflation—was what could be termed a sluggishness as well as an entrenched upward bias to inflation expectations. As articulated by Governor Crow (1988) in his Hanson Lecture, "In my view, the notion of a high, yet stable, rate of inflation is simply unrealistic." Offering the hypothetical example of a central bank tolerating 4 percent inflation, the Governor asserted that a public that sees the central bank as unwilling to reduce inflation from that level would view any shock that moved inflation up (say to 5 percent) as unlikely to be reversed, and therefore likely to be built into inflation expectations. Inflation expectations get an entrenched bias upward when there is no nominal anchor to keep the goal of price stability in view.

The entrenched upward bias of these expectations is cited repeatedly as an empirical reality of the Canadian economy.[1] For expectations to change, Governor Crow argued, the central bank must demonstrate its willingness to pay the costs of disinflating: "But as lower inflation is achieved, as people are less conditioned by fears of inflation, reducing inflation and preventing its resurgence becomes less difficult" (Crow 1989).[2] While this belief explains why the targets announced "provide [a path] for *gradual* but progressive reductions of inflation until price stability is reached" (Bank of Canada 1991c, emphasis added), it begs the question why for three years the Bank

simply declared its commitment to price stability without naming a nominal anchor. It is likely that the Bank was waiting until the elected government was ready to support fully its commitment to price stability (see, for example, Laidler and Robson [1993]).

It is also possible to ascribe to the Bank simply an extended decision-making process that culminated in the opportunity to take advantage of the economic situation of February 1991. The Hanson Lecture itself was ignored in the *Annual Report, 1988*, despite eventually being cited repeatedly in Bank of Canada statements and followed up by "The Benefits of Price Stability" in the *Annual Report, 1990*. An appreciation for the possibilities of targeting seemed to emerge with an even greater lag—in 1989, Governor Crow stated in a speech reprinted in the *Bank of Canada Review*, "In my experience, if [an inflation] target is suggested it is almost invariably whatever the rate of inflation happens to be at the time. Some target!" (Crow 1989, p. 22).[3]

In any event, the decision to adopt inflation-reduction targets was made to "buttress" the Bank of Canada's commitment to price stability and to resolve uncertainties about it (Freedman 1994a). "The targets [were] not meant to signal a shift in monetary policy. . . . All we [were] doing [was] making clear to the public the rate of progress in reducing inflation that monetary policy [was] aiming for" (Thiessen 1991, p. 19). The Bank of Canada did not suggest that the announcement of targets by itself would bring an immediate payoff in terms of reduced inflation expectations; rather, it saw the benefits accruing over a long time horizon. Achieving these targets over the medium term would eventually strengthen public confidence in monetary policy, and inflation control would be supported by the increased transparency and accountability that inflation targets brought to the conduct of monetary policy.

THE OPERATIONAL FRAMEWORK

When announced in February 1991, the Canadian inflation-targeting scheme was a path for reducing inflation defined by three commitments for inflation levels at later dates. (In fact, as mentioned earlier, Bank of Canada officials originally referred to the targets as "inflation-reduction targets.") The first was for 3 percent year-over-year inflation (defined as the change in the CPI) by the end of 1992, twenty-two months after adoption; the second was for 2.5 percent inflation by the end of June 1994; and the third was for 2 percent inflation eighteen months after that.

The Bank stated at the outset that price stability involved a rate of inflation below 2 percent: "A good deal of work has already been done in Canada on what stability in the broad level of prices means operationally. This work suggests a rate of increase in consumer prices that is clearly below 2 per cent" (Bank of Canada 1991c). There was no mention, however, of targeting zero-measured inflation or of a stable price level. The Bank wanted to see further research before committing to a precise operational definition of price stability. It indicated that at the end of 1995, the goal would be a rate of measured inflation of 2 percent, but this rate was not to be considered equivalent to price stability. From the outset of targeting, the Bank made a number of statements to indicate that the correct number for price stability would be defined at a later date, and that there would be further reductions in the target until price stability was achieved. Later Bank studies would estimate the positive-mean bias in inflation measurement of the Canadian CPI to be at most 0.5 percent a year (Bank of Canada 1995, May, p. 4, footnote 1), so more than measurement error must lie behind the Bank's belief in a greater-than-zero definition.

On the appointment of Governor Thiessen in December 1993, the new Liberal Government and the Bank extended the 1 to 3 percent inflation target from the end of 1995 to the end of 1998. The setting of an operational definition of price stability was again put off until more experience was gained about the performance of the economy at low rates of inflation. The Bank specified that it was not treating the current targets as the equivalent of price stability.

There were two reasons for the extension—(i) given that it has been a long time since Canada has had such low rates of inflation, it would be helpful to have more experience in operating under such conditions before an appropriate longer-term objective is determined; (ii) some time is needed to enable Canadians to adjust to the improved inflation outlook.[4] (Freedman 1995)

The Bank attempted in its targets to orient its policies, and public expectations, to forward-looking concerns for the medium term of one to three years, but accepted that expectations and the structures that went with them would not be completely changed (even after three or more years of targeting, and six years by the end of 1998).

The medium-term orientation also informed the Bank's choice of target series. The rate of change in the CPI was chosen as the primary target rate of inflation because of its "headline" quality, that is, it is the most commonly used and understood price measure in Canada. In addition, the CPI had the perceived advantage of coming out monthly, with infrequent delays and without revisions (one alternative, the GDP deflator, is often revised for multiple-observation periods in Canada). Because of the inclusion of food and energy prices in the CPI, however, the series is volatile; to avoid forced responses to short-run blips, the Bank of Canada also uses and reports core CPI, which excludes food and energy, asserting that core CPI and CPI inflation move together in the medium-to-long term.[5] "How we will react [to a change in inflation] will depend on whether or not a change in measured inflation is associated with a shift in the momentum, or underlying trend, of inflation" (Thiessen 1994b, p. 81).

There is no fixed rule by which the Bank is held accountable for performance on either CPI series over a specified time frame, but given the easy observability of these measures, persistent deviations from the path set by the targets would be obvious. Similarly, the Bank of Canada takes out the first-round effects of indirect taxes when determining whether a current or future change in inflation exceeds the target range in a manner that justifies a response.[6] Even allowing for some slow adaptation of price expectations, the targets' distinguishing first- and second-round price effects of shocks are consistent with the Bank behaving in a preemptive manner against inflationary impulses.

Deputy Governor Charles Freedman's discussion of price developments in 1994 illustrates how the Bank uses this combination of factors in assessing the situation:

> In particular, although the 12 month rate of increase in the total CPI through much of 1994 was virtually zero, the Bank focussed on the fact that the reduction in excise taxes on cigarettes in early 1994 accounted for a decline of 1.3 per cent in the total CPI. Operationally, therefore, the emphasis has been placed on the CPI excluding food, energy and the effect of indirect taxes, which has been posting a rate of increase between 1 1/2 and 1 3/4 percent. At mid-1994, the date of the second milestone, the rate of increase of total CPI was at 0.0 percent while that of the CPI excluding food, energy and the effect of indirect taxes was at 1.8 percent, near the bottom of the band. (Freedman 1995, pp. 24-5)

The Bank of Canada makes a strong effort to communicate its reading of the economy and the rationale for its decisions. In doing so, it explains the extent to which the changes in the CPI reflect purely transitory factors or persistent inflationary pressures. The Bank of Canada is very concerned about conveying this message clearly since its target series, CPI inflation, can be sensitive to temporary factors.[7]

As initially announced, inflation would be permitted to range from 1 percent above to 1 percent below each of these targets, and then to lie between 1 percent and 3 percent from 1995 on; but the objective to be targeted was the midpoint. In practice, the Bank never aggressively sought to move inflation from the outer bands toward the midpoints, even when actual inflation lingered at or below the target floor for an extended period. In fact, "in the revised targets more emphasis is placed on the bands than on the midpoints" (Freedman 1995). Explicitly, the target range is intended to allow for control problems.[8] While the Bank recognizes that a band of 2 percent width is indeed narrower than what research has shown to be necessary to capture all the unavoidable variation from unexpected sources, it also felt that too wide a band would send the wrong message (Freedman 1994a).

In general, the belief was that the band would provide sufficient flexibility to deal with supply shocks

that were not already taken care of by exclusion of food, energy, and the first-round effect of indirect taxes.[9] No explicit escape clauses were set up for the Bank of Canada to invoke when larger shocks arose; accommodation of supply shocks (beyond that of referring to core CPI, rather than headline CPI, deviations from trend) was left to the Bank's discretion.

It is important to note how much looser in spirit this target definition is than the Reserve Bank of New Zealand's highly specified list of exceptions, which is dependent upon elected government approval. In many ways, however, the Bank of Canada's definition is a similar operational response to the same difficulties and shocks to which all small open economies exporting a large amount of natural resources are subject. The definition of target inflation in this manner has several implications. First, it commits monetary policy in Canada to reversing shifts in the trend inflation rate, while allowing price-level shifts in the face of supply shocks—it is not a framework consistent with price-level targeting. Second, it grants the Bank of Canada the freedom to act in whatever way it can transparently justify to the public with reference to the target bands; it does not prespecify when the Bank should deviate from target achievement.

Another aspect of the Bank of Canada's framework is that it commits monetary policy to a somewhat counter-cyclical bent, in that the Bank must respond to aggregate demand-driven price increases *and* decreases that would take inflation out of the target range. While common to all inflation-targeting regimes that explicitly or implicitly (in terms of reasonable deviation from a point target) put a floor on inflation goals, this feature has become more prominent and explicit in the Canadian framework:[10]

> Some people fear that, by focusing monetary policy tightly on inflation control, the monetary authorities may be neglecting economic activity and employment. Nothing could be further from the truth. By keeping inflation within a target range, monetary policy acts as a stabilizer for the economy. When weakening demand threatens to pull inflation below the target range, it will be countered by monetary easing. (Thiessen 1996d, p. 2)

The link between developments in the real economy and in prices is not denied by the Bank of Canada despite the focus on inflation goals. Governor Thiessen, in fact, has offered an explanation for inflation distinct from those relating solely to monetary factors:

> Upward pressure on inflation comes about when excessive spending demands in the economy, which are not adequately resisted by monetary policy, persistently exceed the capacity of the economy to produce the goods and services that are being sought. (Thiessen 1995d)

The trade-off between output and prices—even at times when increasing counterinflationary credibility might be expected to reduce the cost of disinflation—explains the gradual way the Bank moved from an initial expected inflation rate of 5 percent at the end of 1991 to a 2 percent target by the end of 1995. Freedman (1994a) noted that a typical augmented Phillips curve equation was broadly able to track the decline in inflation, and that this suggested that there was no need to resort to explanations involving credibility and changes in expectations to explain the pace of disinflation. However, despite the continued output gap, since that time inflation has not fallen further, as these equations predict. One reason for this might be that the process of expectations formation has changed; that is, that the Bank's target is now given substantial weight, such that expectations have been quite firm at about 2 percent.

In any event, the Bank repeatedly holds out the hope in public statements that as private individuals' and firms' expectations adapt, the cost and time necessary to achieve and maintain inflation goals will drop.[11] It is fair to ask, however, how long Canada (or any country) must pursue credible disinflationary, and then counterinflationary, policies before results can be expected. Clearly, in the case of Canada, more than four years of inflation targeting, preceded by at least three years of tightening monetary conditions, were not enough to induce these effects.

Accordingly, the Bank of Canada's justification for the pursuit of inflation targets, and from there price stability, does not rest upon credibility arguments alone. "In other words, our objective is price stability, but as a means to the end of good economic performance rather than as an end in itself" (Thiessen 1994a, p. 85).[12] Interestingly, Governor Thiessen has gone on to extol the benefits of transparency in monetary policy—as fostered by inflation targeting—as a worthwhile pursuit in its own right.

> First, [the central bank] can try to reduce the uncertainty of the public and of financial markets about its responses to the various shocks. It can do this by making clear the longer-run goal of monetary policy, the shorter-term operational targets at which it is aiming in taking policy actions, and its own interpretation of economic developments. Moreover, by committing itself to a longer-term goal and sticking to it, as well as by lessening uncertainty about its own responses to shocks, the central bank may be able to lessen the effect of shocks on private sector behavior. (Thiessen 1995d, p. 42)

No other targeting central bank has so explicitly made a virtue of transparency for its benefit to the economy as well as its role in credibly reducing inflation, although all have made efforts in this direction. Note that the benefits Thiessen lists in this quotation can stem from any sustainable longer run goal of a central bank with a consistent operational framework—neither price stability nor inflation is mentioned. In this context, it is only logical to conclude that the Bank of Canada feels comfortable dealing with various short-run challenges without fear of compromising its longer run goals.[13]

The view of inflation as largely determined by developments in aggregate demand and supply cited above leads naturally to the wide range of information variables the Bank considers when setting monetary policy. From 1982, when M1 was dropped as the Bank of Canada's intermediate target, until 1991, when inflation-reduction targets were announced, the Bank had been actively searching for a substitute among the various broader monetary and credit aggregates, although "[they had] not found the behavior of any one of them sufficiently reliable to shoulder the burden of acting as a formal target for monetary policy" (Crow 1990, p. 36). The move to targeting the goal (or its forecast) rather than an intermediate variable clearly represented a significant paradigm shift. "In our view, underlying inflation is affected primarily by the level of slack in the economy and by the expected rate of inflation," stated Governor Thiessen (Thiessen 1995d, p. 49). Both slack and expectations are factors that cannot be directly observed and that require many related variables to assess. In practice, this has implied that:

> the Bank of Canada has focussed closely on estimates of excess demand or supply (or "gaps") in goods and labor markets as key inputs into the inflationary process. It also follows closely such variables as the rate of expansion of money (especially the broader aggregate M2+ . . .), the growth of credit, the rate of increase of total spending and wage settlements as guides to policy action. (Freedman 1995)

The Bank's May 1995 *Monetary Policy Report*, setting the format for those that followed, discusses product and labor markets, inflation expectations, commodity prices, and the Canadian dollar exchange rate in the section "Factors at Work on Inflation." Monetary aggregates are not mentioned until later in the report, as the last of "other indicators" listed in the "Outlook" section. For measures of inflationary expectations, the Bank considers results from the quarterly survey of the Conference Board of Canada, the forecasts listed in *Consensus Forecasts*, and the differential between the returns on thirty-year conventional and real bonds,[14] but it does not conduct its own surveys.

As an adjunct to the direct discussion of the economic forecast and policy decisions, the Bank of Canada has introduced the concept of a monetary conditions index (MCI) as a short-run operational target.[15] The change in the MCI is defined as the weighted sum of changes in the ninety-day commercial paper interest rate and in the Group of Ten trade-weighted Canadian dollar exchange rate, where the weights are three to one. The three-to-one weighting of interest rate to exchange rate effects on the economy came out of Bank estimates of the six-to-eight-quarter total effect of changes of each upon aggregate demand. The MCI was arbitrarily based at 100 in January 1987, and then computed backward and forward from that point; as a result, the Bank stresses that short-run changes in the MCI are more meaningful than levels.

The fundamental message of the MCI is to remind the Bank and the public that there are two monetary channels affecting aggregate demand in the open Canadian economy at any time. The MCI is therefore a "short-run operational target . . . most useful over a one- to two-quarter horizon" (Bank of Canada 1996, November, p. 21). The MCI is not a nominal anchor in itself, nor does it imply a commitment to intervene to alter exchange rates: "Between quarterly staff projections, the MCI provides the Bank with a continuous reminder that exchange rate changes must be considered when making decisions about interest rate adjustments" (Bank of Canada 1996, November, p. 21).[16] Underlining its tactical role in operations, the MCI is considered only briefly in the published semiannual *Monetary Policy Report*.

The Bank of Canada's *Annual Report, 1994* was a totally redesigned document compared with the 1993 edition. The first item discussed under the heading of monetary policy was the planned introduction of the *Monetary Policy Report*. As opposed to a densely printed, very formal-looking document, the *Annual Report, 1994* (and all those published since) was printed in large type, with extensive use of white space and numerous pictures and graphs. The document was consciously made more user-friendly in tone and distribution as well as in format. As argued in the next section, this change may be seen as part of the Bank's ongoing efforts at public outreach and education, goals that gained greater attention when Gordon Thiessen succeeded Governor Crow. Another factor in the new design may have been the switch in 1995 from "inflation-reduction" to "inflation-control" targets, with the setting of a target inflation level to be maintained.[17] By the Bank's own description, in its *Annual Report, 1994*:

> The new *Monetary Policy Report* will be designed to bring increased transparency and accountability to monetary policy. It will measure our performance in terms of the Bank's targets for controlling inflation and will examine how current economic circumstances and monetary conditions in Canada are likely to affect future inflation. (Bank of Canada 1995a, p. 7)

Governor Thiessen also spoke directly to the reader in an informal manner:

> In carrying out the responsibilities of the Bank, our objective is to promote the economic and financial welfare of Canada. I hope this description of those activities will increase the public's understanding of how the Bank has fulfilled its responsibilities. Communicating what the Bank is up to and why is important if we are going to maintain the confidence of Canadians. This year we have changed the Bank's Annual Report. . . . This new style of annual report is designed to provide more information on what the Bank does, thereby providing a better account of our actions. (Bank of Canada 1995a, p. 5)

This decision was a conscious effort to increase the transparency of policy for the general public. At the time inflation targets were originally adopted, the Bank stated:

> The Bank of Canada will be reporting regularly on progress relative to the inflation-reduction targets and on its monetary policy actions in speeches, in the extracts from the minutes of meetings of the Board of Directors of the Bank of Canada and of course in the Bank of Canada's Annual Report to the Minister of Finance. In addition, an analysis of inflation developments relative to the targets will be published periodically in the *Bank of Canada Review*. (Bank of Canada 1991c, p. 15)

The *Review* switched from monthly to quarterly publication in 1993, however, and the experience of other inflation-targeting countries, particularly the United Kingdom, brought home the utility of a separate publication in eliciting and focusing public discussion.[18]

The semiannual *Monetary Policy Report* has varied slightly in outline in the five issues published to date, but all include some discussion of recent developments in inflation, progress in achieving the inflation-control targets, and the outlook for inflation. To summarize the aim of the *Monetary Policy Report*:

> This report reflects the framework used by the Bank in its conduct of policy. This framework includes: (I) a clear policy objective; (II) a medium-term perspective (given the long lags for the full impact of monetary policy actions on the economy); and (III) a recognition that monetary policy works through both interest rates and the exchange rate. (Bank of Canada 1995, May, p. 3)

The *Monetary Policy Report* is a very user-friendly periodical aimed at the layperson, with "technical boxes" explaining various concepts and procedures in a cumulative fashion (similar to the pedagogical efforts in the United Kingdom's *Inflation Report*). The format emphasizes white space and includes summary bullet points in the margins, and the presentation is limited to less than thirty pages (largely consisting of charts). In addition, the *Report* is made available on the internet or by calling a toll-free number, and a four-page summary (compiling the various summary points) is issued at the same time for those who do not wish to read the entire document. Again, the *Report* represents a major shift in tone and audience from the reporting efforts undertaken in the initial years of inflation targeting in Canada, when the discussion of inflation performance remained in technical language and was bundled with other topics in less accessible publications.

Around the same time, there were some other changes in the internal organization of the Bank of Canada. Most prominently, as summarized in the *Annual Report, 1994*, "the Board of Directors established a new senior decision-making authority within the Bank called the 'Governing Council.' The Council, which [the Governor chairs], is composed of the Senior Deputy Governor and the four Deputy Governors. A major decentralization of decision-making is being implemented in the wake of the Council's establishment" (Bank of Canada 1995a, p. 8). Since this change, all issues of the *Monetary Policy Report* have carried the note "This is a report of the Governing Council of the Bank of Canada" and listed the six individuals' names. The movement to collective responsibility, rather than giving the impression that the Governor embodies the Bank, may be seen as an attempt to increase public perceptions of accountability after Governor Crow had become personally identified with the Bank's policy in the early 1990s.[19]

The Bank of Canada remains a relatively independent central bank.[20] In line with its responsibility for the conduct of monetary policy, the Bank of Canada has full operational independence in the deployment of monetary policy instruments. Thus, the Bank alone determines the setting of policy-controlled short-term interest rates.

Nevertheless, the Bank is subject to the "doctrine of dual responsibility," putting ultimate responsibility for the thrust of monetary policy in the hands of the Minister of Finance, and the Minister can make the Governor follow a particular policy (or move interest rates at a specific time) by issuing a public directive, with which the Governor and the Bank must comply.

A conflict between the Minister and the Bank, however, has never occurred. Because the issuance of a public directive would imply that the Minister had lost confidence in the ability of the Governor to carry out the government's monetary policy, the directive would likely be followed by the resignation of the Governor. Obviously, such a situation would almost certainly have serious repercussions for the government. Thus, a directive would be used only in extraordinary circumstances, and it is not something that can be used routinely by the government to sway the conduct of monetary policy.

Indeed, it might be argued that the existence of the explicit directive power has strengthened the independence of the Bank of Canada, compared with a system in which the procedures for resolving policy conflicts are not spelled out so explicitly. In general, relations between the Finance Ministry and the Bank are quite close. The Minister and the Governor meet almost weekly (though not on a required schedule), the Deputy Minister of Finance holds a nonvoting seat on the Bank's Board of Directors, and there are a number of other less formal contacts as well.[21]

The Bank of Canada's inflation-targeting framework has been an exceedingly flexible one, undergoing constant refinement and development, with a marked trend toward greater transparency over time (discussed in further detail below). The targets changed from "inflation reduction" to "inflation control" of around 2 percent CPI inflation, without commitment to a specific long-run definition of price stability. Furthermore, additional reporting obligations (such as the *Monetary Policy Report*) were undertaken as were new, more transparent operational tactics (for example, the reference to the MCI and the mid-1994 move to target more explicitly an overnight interest rate range of 50 basis points). At the same time, the backward-looking assessment and the forward-looking prediction of the target

inflation series have always been nuanced by reference to developments in core CPI, indirect taxes, and exchange rates, without resorting to a specified rule for how and when to judge success. Finally, the Bank of Canada has become more directly accountable to the public and the markets than to the government directly. In short, the similarity to the German framework[22] and the difference from the New Zealand framework are striking—despite the apparent closeness of the New Zealand and Canadian target definitions and economic situations.

CANADIAN MONETARY POLICY UNDER INFLATION TARGETING

This section summarizes briefly the main events in Canadian monetary policy since the announcement of inflation targets in February 1991. It is based on accounts in the Bank's *Annual Report*s and semiannual *Monetary Policy Report*s (since 1995), speeches and articles printed in the *Bank of Canada Review*, some academic studies, the *OECD Economic Report*s, and various newspaper reports.

The paths of inflation, interest rates, the nominal effective exchange rate (henceforth the exchange rate), GDP growth, and unemployment in Canada depicted in Charts 1-4 (pp. 69-70) indicate that the economic background for monetary policy under inflation targeting can be usefully divided into two basic periods. The first—which ran from the introduction of targets through the end of 1993—was characterized by significant economic adjustment by firms and workers as well as declining inflation rates; at times, headline inflation dropped below the floor of the announced target range. The second—which runs from the announcement on December 22, 1993, when the inflation-targeting framework was extended, to the present—has generally been characterized (except in 1994) by a need to alleviate disinflationary pressures, which have threatened to push inflation below the target range.

One of the challenges that the Bank of Canada faced during these periods was political, rather than economic. The Bank's success in reducing inflation and then maintaining it at a low level was associated by some critics with a high cost in unemployment, although it is by no means clear that the level of unemployment reached at the time was entirely due to monetary policy or that it would have been entirely avoidable if monetary policy had been different. The targeting framework for monetary policy has received support from the public and has thus been endorsed by the two different governments in power since it was first adopted. However, while all central banks that adopted inflation targets received some criticism of their priorities from certain quarters, Canada's critics have probably been the most prominent and vocal in objecting to an exclusive focus on inflation control and to the low level of the target range.

This experience contrasts with that of New Zealand, discussed above, where there was basic agreement that the monetary reforms, including the adoption of inflation targets, were beneficial, but the control problems of the central bank in meeting a tight inflation target band near zero are what drew attention. The Canadian experience also contrasts with that of the United Kingdom, discussed below, where the central bank, because of its lack of independence, did not control the setting of the monetary policy instruments and so was not an obvious target for public criticism. Instead, the primary challenge for policy in the United Kingdom arose from the separation between those accountable for forecasting and assessing inflation performance and those responsible for setting monetary policy.

Accordingly, in this section, we focus upon three critical junctures for the Canadian inflation-targeting framework. The first critical period came in 1991 at the time of the adoption of targets, when forces beyond the Bank of Canada's control—world oil markets and Canadian domestic tax policy—created inflationary impulses. The second came in late 1993 when the Liberal Party won a victory in a federal election with a campaign platform that decried the incumbent Conservative Party's "single-minded fight against inflation."[23] The third came in mid-1996, when the then president of the Canadian Economic Association (and critic of the Bank of Canada) gave voice to a concern about the perceived excessive tightness of monetary policy in the face of high and rising unemployment.

In all three instances, the Bank of Canada responded by directly engaging in substantive discourse and increasing its efforts at transparency and public outreach. The Bank's response should be seen as a success in that the Bank managed to defend its policies without altering its basic commitment to operational price stability. The fact that the Bank effectively won over a sufficient number of wage- and price-setters in the first instance, the Liberal Government in the second, and the general public in the third, demonstrates the potential of inflation targets—and of transparent accountability more generally—to shape and enhance the discussion of monetary policy. With the Bank of Canada's competence and responsibilities clearly defined and tracked, the Bank could justify its policies within a clear structure. Meanwhile, the Bank's critics were forced to argue openly for looser policy on its economic merits (or lack thereof) alone.

The first major challenge to Canadian monetary policy after the joint announcement of inflation targets by Governor Crow and Finance Minister Wilson, on February 26, 1991, was how to cope with contemporaneous upward pressures on the price level. Most important, the Canadian federal government had just introduced a GST along with other increases in indirect taxes by federal and provincial governments. The key for the Bank of Canada's strategy was that these were identifiable, onetime price adjustments with extremely predictable effects *if* the price rises were not passed on by the private sector through a round of price and wage hikes. The Bank had little incentive to raise interest rates, given that it had been pursuing a policy of easing monetary conditions since the spring of 1990, and growth for 1991 was expected to be minimal because of low U.S. aggregate demand and widespread debt overhang in Canada.

The Bank used the targets as a means of communicating to the public that these onetime shocks should not be passed through to trend inflation, keeping the threat of interest rate rises in the background. Looking back from his perspective at the end of 1991, Governor Crow stated in the *Annual Report, 1991*:

> The fact that the economy was able to absorb the GST and the other indirect tax changes without provoking an inflationary spiral—a process of wages

chasing prices, prices increasing further as a result, and so on—has been especially welcome. Certainly, the Bank of Canada has sought to make absolutely clear that monetary policy would not finance such a destructive process. The way that the price effects of the GST have been successfully absorbed has become even more widely recognized with the recent publication of the January 1992 CPI numbers. (Bank of Canada 1992a, p. 9)

In fact, given the tight monetary conditions that had already been established and the unexpected sluggishness of the economy, the Bank was able to ease nominal short-term interest rates 6.5 percentage points between spring 1990 and February 1992, a larger drop than was seen in inflation. Once the tax effects were taken out of the CPI in January 1992, headline CPI inflation dropped to 1.6 percent, while core inflation went from 5 percent in December (still including the GST) to 2.9 percent in January (Bank of Canada 1992a, p. 20).

The Bank's own analysis of the economic situation at year-end 1991 attributed most of the ongoing sluggishness in the Canadian economy to the global slowdown, largely because of debt overhang in the rest of the Group of Seven, as well as low commodity prices for Canadian exports (Bank of Canada 1992a). In January 1992, the Bank announced that it had come in under its expected rate of inflation of 5 percent at the end of 1991.[24] The target success was described in terms of core CPI (that is, excluding food and energy prices) rather than the ultimate target, headline CPI, although both were well below target level (having risen 2.6 percent and 3.8 percent, respectively, over 1991). By February 1992, inflation had already dropped below the target level of 2 to 4 percent for year-end 1992, with core CPI 2.8 percent higher than a year earlier, despite a depreciating Canadian dollar.

The announcement in May 1991 introducing inflation-indexed (real return) bonds, with payments of interest and principal linked to the CPI, served as an additional indicator that the authorities intended to avoid inflationary policies in the future. The announcement was immediately seen (as intended) as an additional incentive for the government and the Bank of Canada to meet the announced inflation targets.[25]

By October 1991, Bank of Canada researchers suggested that Canada had already paid most of the cost of bringing down inflation, as measured by sacrifice-ratio calculations (Cozier and Wilkinson 1991). Some academic economists immediately responded in the press with concern that the Bank of Canada's estimates of the sacrifice ratio were low—possibly by as much as 50 percent.[26] Appealing to a hysteresis-type argument, but also indicating some belief that a persistently looser monetary policy could result in employment gains, these economists predicted that unemployment would remain high. It is important to note that the Bank's response did not include an attempt to deny that disinflation beginning before target adoption involved a cost in terms of real activity—in fact, the release of research on the topic of sacrifice ratios prompted this discussion. Nevertheless, various officials did, at times, hold out the hope that as Canadian inflation expectations adjusted under targets, the cost of future disinflations would drop (see the preceding section).

The debate was therefore about the Bank's policy priority on low inflation, rather than about the framework of targeting itself. This debate over the relative importance of low inflation would become a recurring theme, as we explain below, and the existence of the inflation targets helped to frame the discussion of monetary policy at this general level rather than allowing a conflict over the interpretation of specific policy movements or the competency of policymaking.

There was considerable discussion of the relationship between the Bank of Canada's independence and its inflation-targeting framework in 1991. The Bank of Canada was included in the Conservative Government's proposals for general federal reform published in September; the main changes recommended were to simplify the Bank's legal mandate to emphasize the pursuit of price stability (from its multigoal statement) and to make the Governor's appointment subject to confirmation by the (to-be-reformed) Senate. The Manley Committee in the House of Commons[27] held hearings on the proposals in late 1991, but the government was largely occupied with its agenda of constitutional reforms, then under discussion.

The Bank and others testified that a focused price stability mandate would clarify the accountability of the Bank, whereas it would be possible to defend almost any policy under the current vague mandate. The Committee concluded, however, that "the problem with a mandate narrowly focussed on price stability is that it would tend to enhance the Bank's accountability by reducing unduly the Bank's area of responsibility" (Paragraph 88). In the end, the Manley Committee decided, "The elected government must remain ultimately accountable for the monetary policy followed" (Paragraph 168). In the end, the system of dual responsibility and the old legal mandate were maintained.[28]

By September 1992, the Canadian dollar had fallen to 79 U.S. cents, from 89 U.S. cents a year earlier, and most of the Bank of Canada's activity was concentrated on exchange rate and interest rate interventions meant to slow and smooth the downward trend of both variables. The economy continued to stagnate without falling into recession. The *Annual Report, 1992* noted that the Canadian recovery was much slower than the norm of previous business cycles. Inflation did meet the target on a headline basis, reading 2.1 percent in December, while the 1.7 percent core inflation fell below the target range of 2 to 4 percent. Core inflation would remain between 1.3 and 2 percent until the target path's floor caught up with it in late 1993.

The second critical juncture for the Bank of Canada's targeting framework came in the summer before the November 1993 parliamentary election, when, in light of the unpopularity of the ruling majority and rising unemployment, then Prime Minister Brian Mulroney's Progressive Conservative Party seemed doomed to defeat (although no one foresaw the eventual size of that defeat). The Liberal Party included in its campaign platform a criticism of the Conservative Party's "single-minded fight against inflation."[29] Although the political attack initially focused on the Conservative Party's goals for monetary policy, it sparked debate over whether Governor Crow should be appointed to a second seven-year term when the Liberal Party took office. Market economists did warn the Liberal Party leaders through the press that, if Crow was not reappointed, some other measure would be necessary to

reassure markets of the new government's commitment to low inflation.[30]

In October 1993, preceding the Liberal Party's victory, Deputy Governor Freedman's speech at an academic conference on monetary policy stated:

> With the unexpected sluggishness of the economy, the rate of inflation fell faster and further than initially anticipated, and this despite the fact that monetary conditions were easing for most of the period between the announcement of the targets and the first target date, the end of 1992. . . . [Although inflation was 2.1 percent at the end of 1992, versus a lower band of 2 percent,] it would be inappropriate to push up the rate of inflation once it had reached the lower band of the target range, given that the longer-term goal was price stability.[31] (Freedman 1994a)

On the one hand, this statement underlined both the Bank's unwillingness to engage in fine-tuning (or perceived attempts at it), and its complementary willingness to admit forecast errors and the limits of its control of inflation developments. On the other hand, this stance reaffirmed that the target bands were to be taken more seriously than the midpoint, and it gave the impression that, even then, inflation outcomes that erred on the side of being too low would be accepted.[32] As we saw in the case of New Zealand, as well as in the political pressures on the Bank of Canada, an emphasis upon firm target bands makes explanations of deviations of inflation from the range more difficult to justify publicly because the central bank appears to have already admitted and specified the extent of its required flexibility. The commonly held view is that the deviation must be by the central bank's choice if it is not due to incompetence.

Moreover, a seeming willingness to allow target undershootings for some time even at very low rates of inflation—a possibility also raised by the Bank of England's later interpretation of its target as 2.5 percent *or less*, discussed in Part VI—raises potential economic difficulties resulting from the probable asymmetry of the output-inflation trade-off at very low levels of inflation. More recent statements by the Bank of Canada (cited below), perhaps in reaction to the economic and political experiences we discuss here, emphasize the advantages for policy of having a floor to an inflation target, which, if taken seriously, can help to stabilize output fluctuations.

On December 22, 1993, the new government and the Bank made a joint announcement extending the targeting framework, with the 1 to 3 percent inflation band to be reached by year-end 1995 now extended through 1998. As noted in the previous section, the Bank was careful to indicate that this target remained a medium-term goal, not the achievement of price stability, however defined. It is also worth pointing out that the new Liberal Government saw the need to extend the target beyond its stated endpoint once the change of Parliamentary majority had raised fears about the commitment to the regime. While the Liberal Government could not ultimately guarantee the survival of the commitment beyond the length of its own majority in the House of Commons, it could act to push off the endpoint of the regime toward a more open-ended future, thus removing the endgame pressures discussed earlier in the German case with regard to the run-up to European Monetary Union in Europe.

The Liberal Government elected in October 1993 had campaigned against the single-minded pursuit of low inflation. John Crow chose not to be considered for a second term as Governor, and Deputy Governor Gordon Thiessen was appointed as his successor for a seven-year term beginning February 1, 1994. As noted, on the appointment of Gordon Thiessen, the existing 1 to 3 percent range was extended three more years, that is, until the end of 1998.[33]

In 1994, employment finally rose, largely on the basis of strong export performance. Exports were helped by a declining Canadian dollar, particularly against the U.S. dollar; the Canadian dollar had depreciated for the two years up until the 1993 election and had only temporarily strengthened upon the Liberal majority's reaffirmation of the inflation targets. Interest rates had risen, not only because of U.S. rate increases, but also because of concerns over the Canadian fiscal situation and the high level of political power behind separatism in Quebec. In his last official act as Governor, John Crow used his statement in the Bank's *Annual Report, 1993* (released in March 1994) to call for the reduction of government debt burdens in order to take pressure off interest rates and exchange rates.

Governor Thiessen would make similar statements about fiscal policy in the years that followed, albeit more obliquely to start. In general, inflation-targeting central banks, even independent ones, face a difficult decision in determining what kind of public statements to issue on government fiscal policy. On the one hand, even the most politically neutral inflation forecast, or clear assessment of past monetary policy and inflation performance, requires some estimation of the concurrent fiscal stance and its effects; on the other hand, a central bank that shifts responsibility for outcomes onto the other macroeconomic policy lever or that takes an (actual or perceived) ideological stand on budgetary politics could well undermine its own political legitimacy. Like all the central banks we consider here, the Bank of Canada tended to limit its discussion of fiscal matters to statements about the fiscal stance broadly, its effect on the exchange rate risk premia on interest rates, and general encomiums to the ideals of long-run sustainability.

Over 1994, core CPI inflation had fluctuated between 1.5 and 2 percent, well within the target band. The headline CPI inflation rate had dropped to as low as zero because of a tobacco excise tax reduction in early 1994. Again, the Bank's judicious use of core versus headline CPI to distinguish onetime price shifts from trend largely avoided confusion and the pass-through of first-round effects to wage and price inflation—this time in what would have been a negative direction. Indeed, in February 1995 headline CPI jumped from 0 to 1.8 percent after the first-round effect of the federal and provincial tobacco tax reductions dropped out of the calculations. Since the Bank had already stressed the onetime nature of the preceding price drop (and the stability of core inflation), it felt no need to react to this rise when it occurred (see, for example, Bank of Canada [1995, May]).

Meeting the announced target—and therefore maintaining that target's positive inflation rate rather than driving it toward zero—bolstered the Bank's standing in two ways: it demonstrated the Bank's competence and its reasonableness with regard to the pursuit of price stability. In the *Annual Report, 1994*, Governor Thiessen spoke of the third successive year of "maintenance of a low level of inflation . . . after two decades of high and unpredictable inflation" and remarked on "the progress that has been made towards price stability" (Bank of Canada 1995a, p. 5).

When the first *Monetary Policy Report* was issued in May 1995, the Bank stated in the four-page summary that "core inflation has been consistently within the Bank's inflation-control targets band since early 1993." Year-over-year core inflation had risen to 2.7 percent by that month (its highest level since the end of 1991) and then declined, while headline inflation also peaked at 2.9 percent. After lowering interest rates on three occasions during the summer, the Bank tightened monetary conditions toward the end of the year. First, it raised the overnight interest rate in November and early December 1994 in response to rising U.S. rates and the emergence of strong domestic economic data. Later, it raised rates five times in January and February 1995 to try to stabilize financial markets in the face of a rapid depreciation of the Canadian dollar during a crisis of confidence following the Mexican devaluation. By March 1995, monetary conditions as measured by the MCI were 2 percent tighter because the Canadian dollar had rebounded. Demand for exports was expected to remain strong through the end of 1995, while domestic demand declined in response to interest rate rises and government fiscal restraint. The Canadian economy had grown more strongly than expected in 1994—at a rate of 5.6 percent.

Inflation remained in the upper half of the 1 to 3 percent target band through October, largely because of the prior depreciation of the Canadian dollar.[34] The Bank accepted the inflation performance and its future course, and turned to other short-run concerns. "Throughout the rest of the second quarter [1995], it became increasingly apparent that the economy was not expanding as expected and that an easing of monetary conditions was warranted" (Bank of Canada 1995, November, p. 4).[35] The Bank was willing to admit a forecasting error and to link its monetary policy decisions to real economic developments as long as the inflation target was met. It can be argued that the Bank was able to do so having invested not only in previous credibility-building disinflations, but also in educat-

ing the public in understanding that monetary policy is forward-looking.

The Bank of Canada first cut interest rates 25 basis points in early May, then lowered the operational target for interest rates twice in June, while the Canadian dollar also depreciated. It then cut rates twice more in July and again in August, when the dollar rose. The Bank expected inflation to remain high within the target band until 1996, when "added downward pressure coming from greater-than-expected excess slack in the economy" would bring it into the lower half of the band (Bank of Canada 1995, November, p. 4). Interest rates were cut on October 31, the day after the Quebec referendum on sovereignty failed to pass; in December 1995, headline inflation declined to 1.7 percent, heading into the lower half of the target band and prompting another cut in the overnight interest rate.

When the output gap remained greater than the Bank's 2.5 percent estimate through the first two quarters of 1996, contrary to expectations, monetary easing continued. The overnight rate was cut on January 25 and again on January 31 following a U.S. federal funds rate reduction. Rates were cut once in March and once in April. Since October 1995, the MCI had declined the equivalent of 200 basis points to its lowest level since 1994 (Bank of Canada 1995, November, p. 43). Inflation expectations were unaffected by the loosening and remained at historical lows—the Canadian Conference Board *Survey of Forecasters* and *Consensus Forecasts* both displayed downward trends in two-year-ahead inflation expectations, from around 4 percent in the first half of 1990 to 2 percent in the second half of 1995. The differential between Canadian "real bonds" and thirty-year conventional bonds was 3.25 percent, on par with the smallest differential recorded since the bonds were first issued in 1991.

Most significantly, the Canadian–U.S. short-term interest rate differential turned negative, while the Canadian dollar remained firm, raising hopes at the Bank that Canada's inflation-targeting regime had become such a sufficiently independent source of counterinflationary credibility that the two countries' interest rates might be decoupling. Given the positive effects of these developments on expectations and inflation, and the pressing needs of the real economy, the Bank began to emphasize how seriously it took the floor on its inflation target and the potentially stabilizing effect on real output of so doing.[36]

The third critical juncture for Canadian monetary policy occurred in summer 1996, with the continuing stagnation of Canadian GDP and employment. Criticisms of the Bank of Canada's policies were given more weight because they were delivered by Pierre Fortin, the elected president of the Canadian Economics Association. On June 1, 1996, Fortin delivered a presidential address entitled "The Great Canadian Slump" (Fortin 1996a) to the annual meeting of the Canadian Economics Association. In his address, he characterized Canadian economic performance since 1990 as

a long slide in economic activity and employment . . . [with the] accompanying employment and output losses still accumulating, but . . . they surpass the losses experienced by other industrial countries since 1990. The last decade of this century will arguably be remembered as the decade of The Great Canadian Slump. (Fortin 1996a, p. 761)

After considering and dismissing a number of possible structural explanations for Canada's economic performance, he forcefully argued that the depression of domestic demand was largely attributable to interest-sensitive consumer durables and business fixed-investment demand. "This gives us the clue to the true cause of the great slump of the 1990s: old fashioned monetary and fiscal contraction. I argue that monetary policy has been the leader, and that fiscal policy was *induced* by the monetary contraction" (Fortin 1996a, p. 770).

In Section IV of his address, "Monetary Policy and the Slump," Fortin cites Bank of Canada statements affirming the Bank's control over short-term interest rates and then poses a question:

The only serious question is why the Bank of Canada has kept the short-term real interest rate differential with the United States so large for so long in the 1990s. The answer to this question has two parts: first, since 1989 the central bank has focused exclusively on the goal of zero inflation; second, contrary to expectations, achieving this objective has forced it to impose permanently

higher unemployment through higher interest rates. (Fortin 1996a, pp. 774-5)

The first part of Fortin's explanation is attributed to the Bank of Canada's exclusive focus on inflation, its religious zeal in doing so, and its excessive independence from popular preferences and political control (pp. 775-7). The second part of his explanation is based on his application of the argument of Akerlof, Dickens, and Perry (1996) about a floor for nominal wage changes at or near zero in the Canadian labor markets.[37] If one believes that workers resist nominal wage cuts strongly, whether for reasons of "fairness" or other factors, Fortin argues,

the zero constraint can take a large macroeconomic bite when the median wage change itself is around zero, as was observed over 1992-4. . . . But if inflation is to fall to a very low level, such as the 1.4 per cent of 1992-6 in Canada, and is to stay there, the proportion of wage earners that are pushed against the wall of resistance to wage cuts must increase sharply. The long-run marginal unemployment cost of lower inflation in this range is not zero, but is positive and increasing. (Fortin 1996a, p. 779)

He goes on to state that the Bank of Canada not only has misjudged the output-inflation trade-off at low inflation rates, but also "has displayed a strong deflationary bias that has not reflected the true state of knowledge on the benefits of zero inflation, the true preferences of the Canadian population, and the spirit and letter of the Bank of Canada Act, which reflects those preferences by asking for a reasonable balance between the inflation and unemployment objectives" (Fortin 1996a, p. 781).

Fortin acknowledges that "the Bank of Canada has made every effort at explaining this strategy through public speeches, appearances in Parliament, research papers, *Annual Reports*, and, more recently, *Monetary Policy Reports*. But it is also true that these attempts have more often been exercises in advocacy of a controversial and extreme policy orientation than genuine dialogue with the public" (Fortin 1996a, p. 781). His two primary policy recommendations are to make the Bank of Canada more like the U.S. Federal Reserve System (in his description), with five governors holding staggered terms, and to raise the inflation target's midpoint 1 percent, to 3 percent (Fortin 1996a, p. 781).

In the press discussion that ensued, including Fortin's own summary of his arguments for mass readership, permanent and transitional costs of achieving low inflation were repeatedly confused.[38] Without coming down on either side of the argument, we note that the Canadian–U.S. interest rate differential had dropped along with interest rates more broadly, suggesting that the Bank of Canada was successful in containing inflation. In addition, this suggests that the Bank of Canada had eased monetary conditions because the considerable slack in the real economy implied disinflationary pressures that might cause inflation to drop below the target range. Whether the Canadian economy had borne too great a cost in lost output during the transition process to be justified by the benefits of lower inflation—despite the Bank of Canada's acknowledgments of the cost of disinflation and conscious gradualism documented above—is an issue that merits discussion.

At the time, however, with the public record of the Canadian inflation-targeting framework's goals, actions, and results available for all to see, discussion was limited to debate over the costs and benefits of low inflation and did not address topics of ideology or of competence. This focus forced participants to take an explicit stand (as Fortin did) on defining the goal of monetary policy. The Bank of Canada's response was to articulate further its rationale for the existing 1 to 3 percent inflation target. In a speech to the Ecole des Hautes Etudes Commerciales in Montreal on October 9, 1996, Governor Thiessen put the debate in exactly these terms while addressing Fortin's argument (without mentioning him by name):

> A distinction should be made here between *reducing* inflation and *maintaining* it at a low level. Reducing inflation requires a downward adjustment in inflation expectations and may entail transition costs, which is not the case with simply maintaining low inflation. It is generally agreed that the gains achieved by reducing inflation exceed transition costs when inflation is high. Where opinions are more divided is on the question of how far inflation should be reduced. Some fear that if inflation falls below a certain threshold, the economy will be deprived of a lubricant. . . . I must say that this argument assumes a degree of money illusion that I find difficult to reconcile with the observed

> behavior of wages in inflationary periods. . . . Recent experience will provide us with more useful information in [the wage behavior during periods of slow wage growth]. We have therefore undertaken new research on this question. . . . Since this research is just getting under way, I will confine myself here to reporting that our preliminary examination of the major wage agreements concluded between 1992 and 1994 does not lend evident support to the thesis of inflation as lubricant. (Thiessen 1996d, p. 3)

There are three key points to make about Governor Thiessen's remarks: first, the costs of disinflation are once again forthrightly acknowledged; second, the argument is made on the basis of empirical claims, with the Bank assuming the burden of having to provide supporting (or opposing) research; and third, the discussion is centered on the appropriate level of inflation to target and the pace at which that level should be reached, not on what the goals of monetary policy should be. Later in his remarks, Thiessen attributed the stalling of the expansion in 1994 and 1995 to increased interest rate risk premia due to international market fluctuations and to political uncertainties about Canada. "In such a context [of high interest rates], the benefits of low inflation were slow to be felt" (Thiessen 1996d, p. 7). Referring to the easing of monetary conditions since that time and the decline in the Canadian–U.S. interest rate differential, he stated, "It shows that keeping inflation down is a low-interest-rate policy and not, as some critics have often claimed, a high-interest-rate policy" (Thiessen 1996d, p. 7).

A month later, Thiessen gave another speech responding even more directly to the Fortin argument, titled "Does Canada Need More Inflation to Grease the Wheels of the Economy?"[39] He opened by characterizing

> some ideas you have probably heard about recently. . . . The suggestion is that the Bank, with its focus on bringing inflation down, is largely responsible for Canada's sluggish pace of economic expansion and stubbornly high unemployment in the 1990s. . . . Moreover, in this view, a monetary policy that emphasizes price stability will somehow always be too tight to allow the economy to achieve its full potential in the future. (Thiessen 1996a, p. 63)

After making an extended argument that most of what slowed the Canadian economy in the early 1990s was the combination of externally induced high interest rates and widespread structural change in response to globalization and technical changes, and that the economy was now poised to pick up over the long term, Thiessen made explicit his vision of the relationship between maintaining low inflation and economic growth:

> In fact, when the Bank takes actions to hold inflation inside the target range of 1 to 3 per cent, monetary policy operates as an important stabilizer that helps to maintain sustainable growth in the economy. When economic activity is expanding at an unsustainable pace . . . the Bank will tighten monetary conditions to cool things off. But the Bank will respond with equal concern, by relaxing monetary conditions when the economy is sluggish and there is a risk that the trend of inflation will fall below the target range. (Thiessen 1996a, p. 67)

Having drawn the policy implication of the distinction between disinflating and maintaining low inflation given an announced inflation target, Thiessen then reiterated his belief that the process of wage setting in a low-inflation environment would be flexible enough to allow for occasional wage reductions in industries that required it, thus countering the view that zero inflation would be costly to the economy because of downward nominal wage rigidity.[40]

The purpose of our extended treatment of this third critical juncture in Canadian monetary policy since the adoption of inflation targets is not to give credence to one side of the argument, or even to the existence of the argument itself, but rather to emphasize the form the argument took. The existence of the inflation-targeting framework channeled debate into a substantive discussion about appropriate target levels, with all sides having to make explicit their assumptions and their estimates of costs and benefits while working from a common record of what the goal had been and how well it had been met.

Interestingly, although this argument gave a potentially far better-grounded means of attacking the Bank's stance than that utilized in the 1993 elections, the run-up to the 1997 elections has, in contrast, not included criticism of the Bank of Canada as a major issue. What this difference indicates most of all is that the failure of political accountability claimed by Fortin in "The Great Canadian Slump" address did not exist—rather, this difference indicates that the Bank's form of response, as with previous challenges, had to be through its acknowledged communications efforts. Indeed, the Bank won support through its response, its responsiveness, and its record.

KEY LESSONS FROM THE CANADIAN EXPERIENCE

The Canadian experience suggests that an inflation-targeting framework that shares the ultimate goals of the New Zealand framework but relies on a different operational structure can be highly successful. The key lessons are as follows: First, although some have argued that tight constraints upon or contracts for central banks are necessary to establish counterinflationary credibility, as in New Zealand, inflation has been low under the Canadian inflation-targeting regime, which is characterized by close informal links between the Bank of Canada and the Ministry of Finance and a greater emphasis on accountability to the general public than on meeting specified contracts. Canada's good inflation performance occurred even in the face of negative supply shocks, such as VAT increases and depreciations of the exchange rate induced by fiscal and political developments. Indeed, the Bank's concerted efforts at transparency may have helped the public to distinguish between onetime shocks and movements in trend inflation.

Second, inflation targeting has worked to keep inflation low and stable in Canada even though the inflation-targeting regime is more flexible, similar to Germany's, with misses of the target range less explicitly tied to punishment. This flexibility has allowed the Bank of Canada more room to deviate from the targets when unforeseen shocks occur. As in the German case, a key component of Canada's success with inflation targeting is the Bank of Canada's strong and increasing commitment to transparency and the communication of monetary policy strategy to the general public.

Third, Canadian inflation targeting has been seen by the central bank as helping to dampen business cycle fluctuations, because the floor of the target range is taken as seriously as the ceiling. Indeed, at times, the Bank of Canada has been able to justify easing of monetary conditions in the face of a weak economy by appealing to the inflation targets, with the confidence that this easing would not lead to expectations of higher inflation in the future. Thus, inflation targeting did not force the Bank to forswear all responsibility for stabilization of the real economy.

Chart 1

CORE INFLATION AND TARGETS

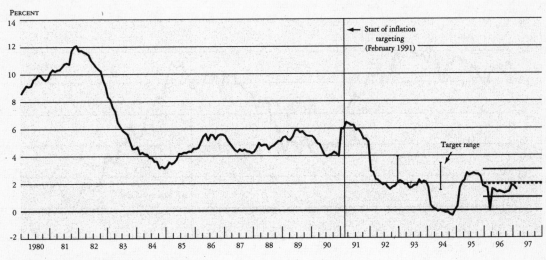

Sources: Bank of Canada; Bank for International Settlements.

Note: The I-shaped bars indicate the target range for inflation in effect before adoption of an ongoing target range of 1 to 3 percent in January 1996; a dashed line marks the midpoint of the ongoing target range.

Chart 2

OVERNIGHT AND LONG-TERM INTEREST RATES

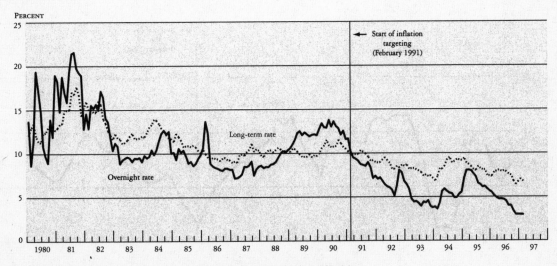

Sources: Bank for International Settlements; International Monetary Fund, *International Financial Statistics.*

Economic Time Line: Canada *(Continued)*

Chart 3

Nominal Effective Exchange Rate

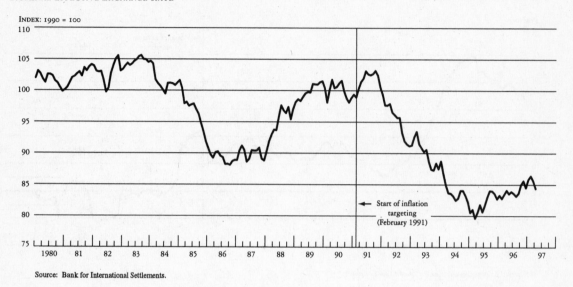

INDEX: 1990 = 100

Source: Bank for International Settlements.

Chart 4

GDP Growth and Unemployment

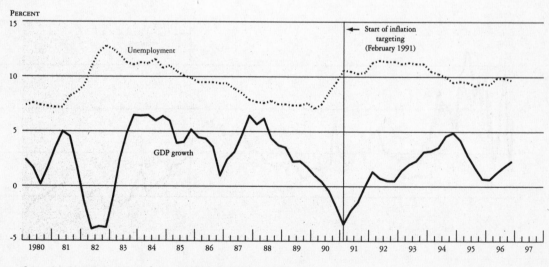

PERCENT

Source: Organization for Economic Cooperation and Development, *Main Economic Indicators*.

Part VI.   United Kingdom

The United Kingdom followed Canada in adopting inflation targeting, but under quite different circumstances. In discussing its experience, we focus on the following themes:

- Like the other countries examined, the United Kingdom adopted inflation targets after a successful disinflation. Unlike these countries, however, the United Kingdom took this step in the aftermath of a foreign exchange rate crisis in order to restore a nominal anchor and to lock in past disinflationary gains.

- In the United Kingdom, there is less attempt to treat inflation targeting as a strict rule than in New Zealand, making the targeting regime more akin to the German and Canadian approach.

- As in the other inflation-targeting countries, monetary policy in the United Kingdom also responds flexibly to other factors, such as real output growth.

- Like Canada, but unlike New Zealand, the United Kingdom separates the entity that measures the inflation target variable (Office for National Statistics) from the entity that assesses whether the target has been met (the Bank of England).

- In the United Kingdom, the headline consumer price index (CPI) is not used in constructing the inflation target variable; the target variable excludes mortgage interest payments, but does not exclude energy and food prices or other adjustments.

- Initially, the Bank of England targeted an inflation range, but then shifted to a point target.

- Because the British central bank lacked independence until the May 1997 election, it was accountable for meeting the inflation targets but did not fully control decisions about the stance of monetary policy.[1] Indeed, up until May 1997, the Bank was limited to providing the principal forecast of inflation and assessing past inflation performance. As a result, the Bank functioned as the Chancellor of the Exchequer's counterinflationary conscience.

- In part because of its weaker position before May 1997, the Bank of England focused its inflation-targeting efforts on communicating its monetary policy strategy and its commitment to price stability, relying heavily on such vehicles as the *Inflation Report*, an innovation that has since been emulated by other inflation-targeting countries.

Although the relationship between the Bank of England and the Chancellor of the Exchequer has now changed, the United Kingdom's targeting framework prior to the granting of independence in May 1997 is an important example to consider in the design of inflation-targeting frameworks in general. (We briefly discuss the post–May 1997 regime at the end of this case study.) In particular, our analysis indicates that the split between the monetary policy decision maker and the primary public inflation forecaster had significant implications for the performance of U.K. monetary policy between October 1992 and May 1997; future actions of the newly independent Bank of England will support or disprove our belief about the importance of this relationship to target performance.

ADOPTION OF THE INFLATION TARGET

The Chancellor of the Exchequer, Norman Lamont, announced an inflation target for the United Kingdom at a Conservative Party conference on October 8, 1992.[2] Three weeks later, at his annual Mansion House Speech to the City (Lamont 1992), he "invited" the Governor of the Bank of England to publish a quarterly *Inflation Report* detailing the progress being made in achieving the target, an invitation that the Governor accepted.

The adoption of a target was an explicit reaction to sterling's exit from the European Exchange Rate Mechanism (ERM) three weeks before. The Chancellor wished to reestablish the credibility of the government's commitment to price stability, which had seemed to gain from the pound's two years in the ERM (as primarily measured by interest rate differentials with Germany and spreads in the U.K. yield curve). Given the United Kingdom's history of trying and abandoning a series of monetary regimes in the post–Bretton Woods period, there was considerable potential for damage to credibility, both at home and abroad, from the aftermath of the Black Wednesday foreign exchange crisis in September 1992 and a currency devaluation of more than 10 percent.

There had been no prior public discussion on the part of either the Treasury or the Bank about setting inflation targets. While the pound was maintaining parity in the ERM, of course, such talk would have been irrelevant because the United Kingdom was committed to attempting to match the Bundesbank's inflation performance. As the exchange rate crisis approached, revealing the existence of a fallback plan could have been dangerous. Accordingly, the announcement of an inflation target of 1 to 4 percent per year in October 1992, unaccompanied by an explanation of the methods for monitoring and achieving this performance, had a certain amount of shock value. Perhaps this approach was seen as underlining the commitment by plunging ahead in a decisive manner. It is important to emphasize that the Chancellor announced the policy adoption at a partisan, though public, forum, and he committed the nation to the targets only "through the end of the present parliament," that is, May 1997. In other words, this was a policy of the ruling Conservative majority, and could not be given a life independent from their own commitment—except to the extent that the framework's success could earn support from the public and opposition parties.

When, in September 1992, the government was faced with the choice between attempting to defend the exchange rate at length (with at least a major downward realignment inevitable) and leaving the ERM, it opted for the latter despite the damage to credibility. The unwillingness of the U.K. monetary policymakers to raise interest rates to defend the currency beyond Black Wednesday—in contrast to, say, Italy or Sweden—suggests that their commitment to the ERM was not very strong.

It thus seems fair to say that the United Kingdom's adoption of an inflation target presented two elements of continuity and one of change with respect to the monetary regime of ERM membership. First and foremost, there was no change in the objective of monetary policy—price stability. The explicitness of this goal and its primacy, however, had increased over the 1990s. By the time the pound exited the ERM, the government had made clear that it did not wish to be let free from discipline, merely from the conflict between German and British business cycles. Second, the strategy followed to achieve this objective had to have credibility with the public through a transparent means of communicating the stance and success of policy.

The main change for the United Kingdom, having abandoned both monetary and exchange rate targets, was the strategic decision not to employ any intermediate target variable in the setting of policy. In fact, in Chancellor Lamont's speech announcing the inflation-targeting policy, he took pains to make clear that money growth and exchange rate measures would be monitored but would not determine policy.[3] A speech delivered by the Bank of England Governor, Robin Leigh-Pemberton, on November 11, 1992, made the point abundantly clear:

> Experience leads us to believe that monetary policy cannot be conducted with reference to a single target variable. The overriding objective of monetary policy is price stability. Therefore policy must be conducted with reference to our expectations of future inflation. . . . Consequently, policymakers should make use of every possible variable, with the importance attached to any given variable at any point in time dependent on its value as a guide to prospective inflation. (Leigh-Pemberton 1992, p. 447)

Thus, targeting the inflation goal directly was seen as the only practical way to achieve the goal. This conclusion, however, still left open the question of how to make this new policy credible, especially after the exit from the visible restraint of the ERM. In his speech, the Governor continued: "But in such an eclectic framework it is possible for the underlying rationale of policy to be lost in a welter of statistical confusion. That is why we have opted for a policy of openness."

This last point, reflecting a belief that efforts at effective ongoing communication with the public—not the announcement of a simple goal alone—are required for credibility, is the operational core of the United Kingdom's inflation-targeting framework. Nevertheless, while the framework emphasizes accountability, the idea that rules have replaced discretion (as in the Reserve Bank of New Zealand's "contract," for example) is not prominent. This may have been more a matter of the reality of ultimate monetary policymaking resting with the elected government rather than of a consciously held conviction. As noted in the discussion of New Zealand, the extent to which inflation targeting is treated as a rule is best seen as a design choice.[4]

The Operational Framework

The intermediate target variable for policy set by the Chancellor and the Bank of England is the annual change in the retail price index excluding mortgage interest payments (RPIX). RPIX was to remain in a range of 1 to 4 percent until at least the next election, with the intent that it would settle itself in the lower half of that range by then (2.5 percent or less).[5] The long-term intended average for RPIX is 2.5 percent or less. RPIX is meant to capture underlying inflation and is usually reported along with RPIY, which is RPIX altered to exclude the first-round effect of indirect taxes. The British have chosen to include the effects of commodity price shocks, including oil shocks, in their target. In all inflation targets other than headline inflation, there is some trade-off between transparency (because headline CPI is what people are accustomed to following) and flexibility (because then onetime or supply shocks are defined out of the target requirement).

RPIX has proved to be an effective measure for the Bank, however, with the financial press and the public adapting to it over time. There was some consideration of a change to RPIY in 1995, but that was seen as switching too often and opening the possibility of being perceived as constantly expanding the list of shocks for which monetary policy would not be responsible. Indeed, to discourage this perception, the Office for National Statistics, an agency separate from the Bank (the forecaster), was asked to calculate the various inflation series (and thus the actual results to be compared with the forecasts).

The target band width, set by the Chancellor, was intended to limit the scope for both slippage and counter-cyclical monetary policy. Later interpretations by the Bank and the U.K. Treasury, however, indicate that it was never intended as a range strictly speaking, but as an admission of imperfect control.[6] Once set, however, the band width takes on a life of its own, so that widening the band would likely be seen as a loosening of policy or a failure to keep the commitment.

The official position agreed to by the Treasury and the Bank in recent years is that there is no longer an actual range for the target, but a point target of 2.5 percent to be met on an ongoing basis. This change was made explicit in Chancellor Kenneth Clarke's (1995) Mansion House Speech to the City on June 14, 1995.[7] In reality, the end-point of such a time horizon is likely to correspond to the lifetime of any parliamentary majority, as it did in New Zealand when the country changed its target range after the October 1996 election. Unlike New Zealand, however, the United Kingdom makes no explicit commitment to remain within a range. Therefore, the U.K.'s inflation point target allows flexibility by permitting short-run unavoidable deviations while shifting the focus away from the values of the bands themselves.

Another issue inherent in the United Kingdom's targeting framework was the tying of the endpoint of the target period to a specific event—the end of the then-sitting Parliament. Unless the commitment to inflation targeting is open-ended, there is uncertainty about whether the targeting regime will continue past the close of the designated period. As a result, there may be increasing doubts about the country's will to undertake necessary actions to meet the targets as the end of the period approaches and pressures increase to let bygones be bygones. As noted in the discussion of German monetary targets in the run-up to European Monetary Union (EMU), these doubts and pressures will arise for any targeting framework that is not renewed far ahead of its announced (or politically determined) endpoint. Just as the Liberal majority in Canada, shortly after taking office in 1993, extended the 1995 targets to 1998, the British Labour Party made clear that it would extend the inflation target of 2.5 percent or less for the duration of its tenure in office should it win in May 1997, thereby removing a potential source of uncertainty and lowering credibility.[8] In contrast, in the New Zealand elections of October 1996, there was no way to shield the time horizon of the targets from the political process. This difference may, in part, have been related to the formal agreements tightly tying the Reserve Bank of New Zealand's goals to the majority in government.

In reality, the actual target of Bank of England policy is the *expectation* of RPIX inflation in the domestic economy. The success in meeting the target is judged by whether the Bank's own inflation forecast over the next two years falls within the intended range. This approach to assessing success is consistent both with a forward-looking orientation and a belief that it takes about two years for monetary policy to affect inflation. At the time of the Chancellor's initial announcement of the adoption of targets, he was criticized by market observers for focusing on a lagging indicator by targeting RPIX inflation per se.

From the first *Inflation Report* onward, the Bank has increasingly considered private sector inflation forecasts and their spread in addition to the distribution of the Bank's own inflation forecasts. In recent issues of the *Inflation Report*, this focus has shown itself in discussions emphasizing the skew of forecast distributions as opposed to a point estimate or even confidence intervals.[9] Most important, the Bank does appear to have successfully communicated to the press and the public that a forward-looking monetary policy must be designed to achieve a balance of risks rather than tight control (even with lags considered). Since many central banks have this intellectual framework behind their policymaking, there is much to be appreciated in the Bank's efforts in this direction.

The Bank of England does appear to be working

from a standard policy feedback framework in line with the Chancellor's and Governor's initial speeches—that is, one in which all pieces of information are gathered and weighed. M0 and M4 (narrow and broad money) figures must be reported, with "monitoring ranges" announced for them, but with an explicit escape clause indicating that when their information conflicts with RPIX forecasts, the RPIX forecasts are to be believed. Exchange rates and housing prices have been repeatedly cited as other indicator variables in the policy decisions by the chancellors and governors over the period, but with the pointed absence of any explicit ranking of the usefulness of different indicator variables. The Bank acknowledges that its failed experiences with money and exchange rate targeting have made it hesitant to rely on the stability of any one indicator or relationship.

The stated ultimate goal of the United Kingdom's inflation targets is price stability, "namely that the rate of inflation anticipated by economic agents is unimportant to savings, investment, and other economic decisions" (Leigh-Pemberton 1992). As in most other countries, a target of zero inflation was dismissed as unduly restrictive given the failure to capture all quality adjustments in price indexes (although the Bank of England points out that RPIX is rebased far more frequently than in many other countries, so there would be less substitution bias for the United Kingdom's price index). Consequently, price stability is operationally defined as growth in RPIX of 2.5 percent or less. The choice of this figure was primarily a pragmatic decision, with the likelihood that if the 2.5 percent goal were achieved and maintained, a lower goal, say of 2 percent, would then be set. No consideration of any other goals, such as exchange rate stability or business cycle smoothing, is explicitly acknowledged within the target framework.

Like every other central bank, however, the Bank of England remains de facto committed to trading off disinflation when necessary against its real-side costs and its effects on the financial system. This is best illustrated by excerpts from Governor Leigh-Pemberton's November 1992 speech about the policy shift, "The Case for Price Stability." The speech, reprinted in the Bank of England's

Quarterly Bulletin, states, "The overriding objective of monetary policy is price stability." In the preceding paragraph of the speech, however, the Governor explains why other factors *overrode* that objective and prompted the pound's exit from the ERM:

> It [the ERM] certainly offered a very visible sign of our commitment to price stability . . . [but] there was a real risk of these disinflationary forces doing quite unnecessary damage to the real economy. Although we would have achieved price stability very quickly—indeed there is reason to believe we might have reached that position during 1993—there was a real danger that the deflation which was already apparent in certain sectors of the economy (notably asset markets) would have become much more widespread. It was not necessary to compress the transition phase to price stability into such a short time span and could well have been counterproductive in the longer term.[10] (p. 446)

This trade-off is recognized even in contexts where the choice between achieving an inflation goal quickly at a high cost in real output or more slowly at lower cost is less stark than that presented by the divergence of German and British domestic needs within the European Monetary System (EMS) in 1992. Why else would the achievement of price stability be pursued gradually, as outlined by the Bank and the Chancellor for the path from the September 1992 RPIX rate of 3.6 percent? Clearly, a gap exists between the claims and reality of inflation as a sole goal even under inflation targeting.[11] Various speeches by Governor Eddie George in recent years have been at pains to stress that the Bank aims to stabilize the business cycle (and thereby at least partially engender exchange rate stability) within the target constraint.

Only three weeks after the decision to adopt inflation targeting, Chancellor Lamont coordinated with the Bank of England an institutional implementation of the policy. The Bank would produce its own inflation outlook on a quarterly basis, beginning with February 1993; the Bank's medium-term forecast for inflation would be the main yardstick of success or failure. As mentioned above, the role of this forecast in accountability for policy becomes quite complicated. One complication arises when interest rate decisions are inconsistent with the implications of the published forecasts, but a full explanation for the rationale behind the decision is not made public. Nevertheless, the rapidity with which the commitment to publish forecasts was undertaken underlines just how central communication efforts are to the operation of the United Kingdom's inflation targets—and how the announcement of the targets was never thought to be enough on its own.

As part of its role in tracking progress toward the inflation target, the Bank of England's *Inflation Report* details past performance of the U.K. economy, compares actual inflation outcomes (both RPIX and its components) with prior forecasts of the Bank, identifies factors presenting the most danger to price stability, and forecasts the likelihood that inflation will in two years' time be in the target range. In the words of Governor Leigh-Pemberton (1992), "Our aim will be to produce a wholly objective and comprehensive analysis of inflationary trends and pressures, which will put the Bank's professional competence on the line." From the third issue (August 1993) onward, the *Inflation Report* has consistently followed a six-part format covering developments in inflation, money and interest rates, demand and supply, the labor market, pricing behavior, and prospects for inflation. In addition, the *Inflation Report* does not supplant the ongoing publication of policy speeches and relevant research in the *Quarterly Bulletin*, in which the authors of the research articles are always identified.

The transparency of the Bank's views and the Chancellor's reaction to them is meant to be the check on the government's monetary stance between elections. Following the third *Inflation Report* in August 1993, it was decided that the Bank would only send the report to the Treasury after it had been finalized. Thus, the Treasury would have no chance to edit or even suggest changes. This agreement on timing indicates the government's conscious acceptance of the Bank's distinct voice.

The *Inflation Report* is best seen in the context of the Bank's traditional role as adviser to the Chancellor on monetary policy. Even after the adoption of inflation targeting, the Bank's contribution remains that of advice and information, just as it had presumably been consulted on Chancellor Lamont's initial decision to implement inflation targeting and the choice of target range and midpoint.

What is innovative is the fact that the Bank would be called upon to report to the public independently of its regular consultations with the Treasury staff and with the Chancellor directly. Often overlooked, however, is the fact that the Treasury, which reports directly to the Chancellor, was commissioned to produce its own monthly monetary report from December 1992 onward. This publication, which predates the *Inflation Report* and is issued more frequently, had a mandate to track the growth of broad (M4) and narrow (M0) money in the monitoring ranges set by the Chancellor and to keep readers apprised of moves in the foreign exchange and asset markets, particularly U.K. housing. In other words, the Chancellor committed U.K. monetary policy to the monitoring of a particular set of indicators compiled by his own staff, even if the Bank of England chose to emphasize other variables or compute numbers differently. The Bank, despite the *Inflation Report*, has not been given a monopoly on monetary policy advice.

The emphasis on public explanations of policy, and especially on delineating differences between the Chancellor's and the Bank's points of view, was buttressed by three additional institutional changes. First, in February 1993, the monthly meeting between the Chancellor and the Governor to set monetary policy was formalized. Second, starting in November 1993, the timing of any interest rate changes decided upon by the Chancellor at the monthly meeting would be left to the Bank's discretion as long as the changes were implemented before the next meeting. Combined with the Bank's commitment to issue a press release explaining the reason for any interest rate change once made, this discretion gave the markets a great deal of information about the Bank's view of the Chancellor's decision. Third, and most significant, since April 1994, the minutes of the monthly Chancellor-Governor meetings have been publicly released two weeks after the next meeting (replacing the prior lag of thirty years with one of six weeks).

In essence, the Bank has operated as the government's institutional counterinflationary conscience. There was an underlying tension in this role because the Bank remained under the control of the Chancellor while the instruments of monetary policy remained out of its control. The Bank's use of public and formalized forums to commu-

nicate its forecasts, its analyses, and even its explicit monetary policy recommendations does increase the cost for the government of going against the Bank's assessment and thus, presumably, of not serving price stability. Unfortunately, since the Chancellor did not have a requirement to report his reasoning beyond what he chose to reveal at these monthly meetings, disputes over preference or competence can become shrouded as competitions over forecast accuracy (see next section).

The standing given the Bank by the monthly minutes did not, however, provide monetary policy with democratic accountability beyond that given already by elections; it was the Bank, not the market or the people, that was passing judgment, but any punishment or reward for that judgment (beyond market reactions) had to wait until the next election. Even under the new Monetary Policy Committee of the Bank, which sets U.K. monetary policy, ultimate responsibility for the goals and outcome of policy rests with the parliamentary majority at the next elections.[12] Nor did these forums provide clarity about the intent of ultimate policy, since, for all the Bank's statements, the Chancellor could override them with only limited public explanation.

BRITISH MONETARY POLICY
UNDER INFLATION TARGETING

This section summarizes briefly the macroeconomic outcomes and the interaction between the Treasury and the Bank at critical junctures in the policy-setting process since target adoption. The section draws on various issues of the Bank's quarterly *Inflation Report* and on the Minutes of the Monthly Monetary Meetings between the Chancellor and the Governor. To support this review of monetary policy, Charts 1-4 (pp. 84-5) track the path of inflation, interest rates, the nominal effective exchange rate (henceforth the exchange rate), GDP growth, and unemployment in the United Kingdom both before and after inflation targeting was introduced.

The period from October 1992 until the end of 1993 was marked by the beginning recovery of the U.K. economy. Sterling's exit from the ERM coincided with the end of recession. GDP growth turned positive in the first quarter of 1993, and the unemployment rate peaked at 10.6 percent in December 1992 (Chart 4, p. 85). Throughout 1993, output growth was accelerating, and the unemployment rate declined. With some brief interruptions, RPIX inflation continued its downward trend, reaching the midpoint of the designated target range of 2.5 percent for the first time in November 1993 (Chart 1, p. 84). The exchange rate bottomed out in February 1993, then strengthened through the remainder of the year (Chart 3, p. 85).

Two major themes in the medium-term inflation forecasts of the first two issues of the *Inflation Report* (February and May 1993) are the inflationary impulses from sterling depreciation and the growing government budget deficit. The official interest rate (the *base rate*) had been reduced from 10 percent in August 1992 to 6 percent in January 1993 (Chart 2, p. 84), reflecting the desire to escape from German monetary tightness. Unsurprisingly, between the United Kingdom's exit from the ERM and early February 1993, sterling had depreciated by 14.5 percent.[13] In explaining why inflation expectations might still be above the target range, the Bank mentioned fears of *eventual* monetization of the unsustainable debt. The Bank did not make any call for immediate fiscal action or actively criticize the government's stance. The Bank's inflation projections in the first two reports continued to fall at all horizons discussed.

In the May 1993 *Inflation Report*, the Bank stated that it believed that the government would manage to hold inflation below 4 percent for the following eighteen months. This statement did not represent an endorsement of the government's monetary stance: not only had the Chancellor committed to being within the inflation range (that is, below 4 percent) in two years, but he had also stated that he would have inflation in the lower half of that range (below 2.5 percent) by 1997. It is interesting that the Bank felt comfortable tracing the source of inflation risk to the government's decisions (suggesting that it was a matter of the government's choice), rather than to economic risks. The Bank expressed concern about the exchange rate's potential effects, noting that the 5 percent appreciation of sterling (trade-weighted) since February permitted only a small measure of optimism, but surveys

and financial market interest rates continued to indicate a lack of medium-to-long-run credibility. The Bank also emphasized that the principal uncertainty about the inflation forecast, most of it on the upside, had to do with domestic wages and profits. The meaning of these concerns became clear three weeks later when Governor George gave a speech explicitly warning against a rate cut. The Bank apparently feared that with the imminent change in chancellors (from Norman Lamont to Kenneth Clarke) and submission of the budget, a decision to ease would be made in compensation for various fiscal measures. At the time, rates were not cut.

Six months later, in the November *Inflation Report*, the Bank touched on the same themes but even more sharply. There was a slight probability now, according to the Bank, that inflation would exceed the target in the near term. Moreover, the Bank said it foresaw real potential for a wage push if headline inflation were to be allowed to rise up to the 4 percent target band. Again, the Bank was responding to a political situation in which many Conservative Party backbenchers and commentators were expecting an interest rate cut. The government had agreed to certain spending cuts and an extension of the value-added tax (VAT) to domestic fuel and power starting in April 1994, while economic real-side news was generally not good. This time Chancellor Clarke did lower rates 3/4 percent without further fiscal tightening to compensate.

What made this conflict between Bank and Chancellor particularly interesting was that the Bank had already offered an out for the Chancellor in the May and November issues of the *Inflation Report*. The Bank attributed 0.4 percent of the projected rise in inflation in 1994 to the VAT change, which it was sympathetic to in general terms as a deficit reduction, and reminded people that if RPIY (which excludes the first-round effect of taxes) rather than RPIX were considered, the inflation would be on target (albeit near the top of the range and with upside risks). For whatever reason, the Chancellor did not take advantage of the proffered defense.

Though unexercised, this sort of definitional tactic raises a real dilemma for accountability. If indirect taxes are legitimately to be excluded, why did the Chancellor and the Bank choose to target RPIX and not RPIY in the first place? If the government had in fact switched to RPIY after the Bank had "allowed" (that is, explained without criticizing) the move, how could the markets and electorate have been sure this was not just a onetime escape clause? And if the wage spiral the Bank worried about sparking tends to run on headline inflation, would this switch have been beside the point, or would it have allowed a shift of blame to the unions' lack of sophistication? On the basis of this case, it would appear that the people who set the definitions of the inflation measures should be kept separate from the people who assess success in achieving them. The United Kingdom's framework might be compared with New Zealand's on this score: New Zealand's central bank—partly because of the country's small size—retains some amount of discretion over the short-run definition of the target inflation series and, on a few occasions, has exercised it.

Around the beginning of 1994, against the background of the better than expected inflation performance, the Chancellor eased monetary policy further. Inflationary pressures remained subdued as the lagged effect on prices of the earlier depreciation was offset by a reduction in unit labor costs related to continued weak employment. It was apparent at the time that pass-through of the onetime drop in the exchange rate upon ERM exit had been effectively averted—a major success for the new monetary regime.[14] This triumph was even more impressive than the Bank of Canada's successful avoidance of passing through a onetime rise in taxes in 1991, given that it followed a presumptive blow to U.K. credibility upon the country's exit from the ERM. The base rate, which had been reduced from 6 percent to 5.5 percent in November 1993, was cut to 5.25 percent in February 1994. These rate reductions occurred despite projections in every *Inflation Report* from August 1993 on that inflation would rise until the end of 1995. Indeed, actual inflation did not start to rise until the end of 1994.

When assessing its past predictions, the Bank repeatedly mentioned slow earnings growth and a squeeze in retail margins as reasons for the unexpectedly low inflation outcome. Although cast as a difference over the implications of incoming economic data, the divergence between the Bank's opinion and the Chancellor's policies

could, in our view, reflect differing assessments of the importance of achieving the inflation target in the short run. Indeed, as long as the elected official can appeal to differences between his or her own private forecast and the central bank's published forecast, the official can hide what is actually a weaker commitment to the stated inflation goal. We find this pattern again in the next situation we consider.

Throughout 1994, GDP grew vigorously, with fourth-quarter GDP exceeding the previous year's by 4 percent. For the first ten months, RPIX inflation was trending downward, reaching a twenty-seven-year low of 2 percent in September and October before it started to rise to 2.5 percent in December. The unemployment rate fell further during the year, to around 9 percent. Sterling (according to the Bank's index) had peaked at the end of 1993 and trended slightly downward during the year.

During the summer of 1994, it became clear to the Bank that the economy was rebounding more strongly than expected, and the *Inflation Report* began to cite evidence of inflationary pressures (for example, growth in wholesale prices). Despite the still-improving inflation performance—both RPIY and RPIX inflation at the time were below 2.5 percent and falling—the Chancellor, on the advice of the Governor, raised the base rate on September 12, and again on December 7, by 0.5 percent each time. Unlike the previous tightening in 1988, these base rate increases were preemptive—a fact that was widely noted in the press.[15] The ability to tie current policies to a future priority, and to justify those policies as acting with a lag, appears to be one advantage of having a specified medium-term goal consistent across targeting regimes.

The discussions between Chancellor Clarke and Governor George during the time leading up to the September 1994 tightening offer some insight into the role that the Bank's medium-term inflation forecasts play in the policy-setting process. During their meeting on July 28, the Governor pointed out that, on the basis of the Bank's latest forecast,

> he did see a risk to the inflation objective in 1996, implying a need to tighten policy in some degree before very long. . . . He was not, on the current

best guess, forecasting a strong upturn in inflation, and there was, as always, a significant margin of error around that best guess. But the best guess for mid-1996 was already slightly above the mid-point of the target range, and there was an uncomfortable sense that the upside risks to the medium-term forecast might, this time, be somewhat greater than the downside risks.[16]

The Chancellor, however, remarked that "there was a danger of trying to set a game plan too far in advance and not looking at the actual evidence as it unfolded. . . . The forecasts suggested inflation might be even lower in the next few months."[17] Although agreement was reached not to raise interest rates at that time, this decision made ambiguous the extent to which monetary policy decisions were indeed based on the Bank's medium-term forecast. While the existence of target commitments, and the Bank's open statements of opinion, moved the U.K. government toward a more forward-looking monetary policy, the government could not be forced into the policy that the Bank considered optimal. Again, the government's private forecast—even if driven as a politically motivated markdown from the Bank's formal analysis—became the actual target. Moreover, because both the estimate itself and the reasoning behind it were not shared with the public, the government forecast could not fully serve as a transparent target.[18]

During 1995, GDP growth decelerated, from 4 percent between the fourth quarter of 1993 and the fourth quarter of 1994, to 2 percent by the last quarter of 1995. The unemployment rate continued its gradual downward trend, reaching 8 percent at year's end. RPIX inflation rose to 2.8 percent in January, and for the rest of the year fluctuated between 2.6 percent and 3.1 percent without exhibiting any trend. Early in 1995 it became apparent that output growth, although slightly slower than in early 1994, was still running high relative to potential, and that observation contributed to the Bank and the Chancellor's belief in a worsening inflation outlook. Consequently, on February 2, the base rate was raised 0.5 percent, to 6.75 percent. Despite this preemptive interest rate increase, the exchange rate fell steeply over the three months following the February increase. By

May 4, the Bank of England's sterling index was down 4.7 percent from February 2. The depreciation was seen to aggravate the discrepancy between the recovery in the tradables sector and that in the nontradables sector, a discrepancy that became increasingly evident at this time. This "dual economy" was highlighted by the contrast between 10 percent growth in export volumes during 1994 and flat retail sales and falling earnings growth in services during early 1995.

As a consequence of the depreciation and the resulting increase in import prices, the Bank's RPIX inflation projection in May 1995 was revised upward nearly 1 percent throughout 1996 from the February forecast, with RPIX inflation reaching almost 4 percent in the first half of 1996 before falling to around 2.5 percent in early 1997.[19] The potential consequences of the exchange rate development for the inflation outlook completely dominated the discussion during the monthly meetings on April 5 and May 5. At least indirectly, this discussion informed the public that the pass-through to inflation from exchange rate movements was faster than that from either output or interest rates.

It was against the background of this upward revision of the Bank's inflation forecast and the dual economy mentioned above that in their meeting on May 5, 1995, the Chancellor overruled the Governor's advice to raise interest rates. This refusal of Chancellor Clarke to raise rates provides an even starker example of the conflict (and the difficulties in assigning accountability) arising from the Bank of England's dependent status than the November 1993 episode discussed earlier. At the end of that day's monthly meeting with Governor George, Chancellor Clarke immediately summoned the press and announced that he was leaving rates unchanged; since, contrary to custom, the Governor was not present to echo the Chancellor's post-meeting statement, and Clarke gave some details of the discussion (including some of George's reasons for concluding that inflation was a real threat) rather than waiting for release of the minutes six weeks later, it was clear that Clarke was overruling the Bank.[20] Clarke cited his personal skepticism about the incoming and forecasted U.K. growth numbers but seemed to be as intent on making the conflict apparent as on explaining it (Chote, Coggan, and Peston 1995).

Perhaps this candor from Chancellor Clarke was a response to the new strength granted the Bank through the inflation-target-reporting framework: facing this reality, Clarke may have felt that the best defense was a good offense. The conflict would have been confirmed with the release of the Bank's May *Inflation Report* a week later. The Bank's central estimate was for 3 percent inflation in two years' time, indicating that, contrary to the government's pledge, inflation would be in the upper half of the target range at the end of the sitting Parliament. Furthermore, the Bank added that the risks to its forecast were almost uniformly on the upside and that these risks were "large." The Bank explicitly noted that sterling was depreciating as it had in the fall of 1992, but that, unlike then, wage and capacity pressures were high.

Upon taking office, Chancellor Clarke had made a commitment to Governor George that he would not censor the *Inflation Report* at any time, but in return he reserved the right to say he disagreed. What seems to have emerged as accountability for policy decisions in this framework is a system in which the Chancellor has to make explicit his or her independence from the Bank of England's position when a disagreement exists, and to make some modest effort to justify the rejection of the Bank's inflation forecast. As suggested above, however, while this system may have a salutary effect on the overall counterinflationary stance of policy, it may undermine public trust in the competency and objectivity of forecasting and of policymaking, and may even obscure what the actual forecast is.

Over the following months, it became apparent that the Chancellor had guessed right as a forecaster. GDP first-quarter growth was revised downward, new numbers on housing and manufacturing came in below expectations, and the global bond market rally (surrounding the expected drop in U.S. interest rates) supported the pound. In a September 1995 account of the Chancellor-Governor discussions since May, Governor George reiterated that "we still think that the chances are against achieving the inflation target over the next 18 months or so without some further [base rate] rise," but he conceded that "we are not

in fact pressing for one—and have not been doing so since before the summer break" (George 1995a).

So should the Bank be taken to task for being less accurate in forecasting than the Chancellor ex post in this one instance? Since the Chancellor's private forecast of May 1995 remained private in number and reasoning, at least in comparison with the *Inflation Report*, it again proved impossible to determine whether Clarke disagreed with the Bank because he was skeptical of the growth forecasts, or simply because he was willing to take a risk of greater inflation to achieve higher growth. Would a point-by-point rebuttal of the *Inflation Report*, however, have been worth the additional information given the damage it might have done to perceptions of the Bank's forecasting role? A record of forecast performance clearly matters for accountability; equally clearly, however, reducing the monetary policy debate to a Chancellor-Bank forecasting competition is undesirable. This tension appears to be inevitable as long as the transparent (and intended-to-be-persuasive) forecast and the interest rate decisions come from different sources.

The minutes of the meetings do not provide any clear answers to these questions but accentuate the issues. Specifically, the minutes give the impression that the subject of discussion between the Governor and the Chancellor is never the stated reasoning behind the Bank's medium-term forecast itself, but rather whether the most recent data that feed into the forecast represent an underlying trend or are distorted by some contemporaneous event. The minutes of the discussion during the June 7, 1995, meeting state that "while one strength of the policy process was that all the new evidence was examined each month for its implications for inflation, it was important not to read too much into one month's data which could prove to be erratic."[21] This sort of discussion might be construed as undermining the importance of the Bank's medium-term forecast.

On June 14, 1995, in his Mansion House Speech to the City, Chancellor Clarke (1995) extended the announced inflation target beyond the latest possible date of the next general election. The Chancellor did admit, however, that inflation could well temporarily rise above

4 percent, the top of the target range, in the following two years; he also left some confusion about whether meeting the target entailed being below the 4 percent ceiling or below the 2.5 percent target set by him and his predecessor for the end of this Parliament. Governor George (1995b), in his speech to the same audience, referred only to the 2.5 percent target, calling it achievable. Inflation expectations at a ten-year horizon, as derived from government bond yields, then rose upon these remarks, from 4.36 percent in early May to 4.94 percent in late July, a move that only in late 1996 began to be reversed.

The Bank's inflation outlook during the second half of 1995 was shaped by weighing the upside risks to inflation resulting from the lagged effects of the earlier sterling depreciation against the downside risks from increasing signs of slowing output growth and a buildup in inventories, particularly during the second quarter of 1995. Domestically generated inflation pressures remained weak, with tradables inflation continuing to outpace that of nontradables. In addition, the Bank noted in its November *Inflation Report* that during the current cycle, real wages had been much more subdued than expected. Still, RPIX inflation, at 3.1 percent in the year to September, was forecast to peak at about 3.5 percent during the first half of 1996. Substantial downward revisions of GDP figures for the first three quarters of 1995 and an unexpectedly low RPIX inflation rate of 2.9 percent in the year to November set the stage on December 13 for the first of four successive quarter-point cuts in the base rate.

The hoped-for "soft landing" of the U.K. economy materialized in 1996. GDP growth picked up toward the end of 1996; in the third quarter, GDP was up 2.4 percent over its level for the third quarter of 1995. The unemployment rate continued its gradual decline, dropping to 6.7 percent by December 1996. From October 1995 to September 1996, RPIX inflation fluctuated only between 2.8 percent and 3 percent, then rose to 3.3 percent in October and November. From January to the end of September, sterling strengthened gradually from 83.4 to 86.1 according to the Bank's exchange rate index, then finished the year in a rally at 96.1, an appreciation of 11.6 percent over three months.

Receding cost pressures and weak manufacturing output data, as well as a GDP figure of 0.5 percent, for the last quarter of 1995 prompted the next two quarter-point base rate cuts on January 18 and March 8. At their March 8 meeting, the Chancellor and the Governor agreed that demand and output were likely to pick up later in the year and through 1997, and that there was a possibility that the latest rate cut would have to be reversed at some point. Again, given the credibility of the Bank of England's role as the Chancellor's counterinflationary conscience, the Bank granted the Chancellor a de facto escape clause—or at least justification of future reversals as necessary and not reflective of a shift in preferences—when the Bank supported the Chancellor's interpretation of the economy. In May 1995, a similar defense had been offered, but not used; this time the option was exercised by mutual agreement.

The Bank's assessment did not change during the spring, and its medium-term projection published in the May *Inflation Report* was essentially unchanged from the previous one. The central projection of RPIX inflation in two years remained at 2.5 percent, with the risks biased downward over the short term but upward over the medium term because of uncertainties concerning the strength of the expected pickup in activity. Following the June 5 meeting, the Chancellor announced another quarter-point cut in the base rate despite the opposition of the Governor, arguing that the cut "was sufficiently small not to cause any significant inflationary risk, while reducing the downside risks to the recovery. If consumer demand started growing too strongly, and put the inflation target at risk, the rates could be raised when this became evident."[22] In this instance as in those discussed earlier, there appears to be some tension between the Bank's forward-looking approach based on its projections and the Chancellor's tendency to emphasize the current economic situation and the latest data. With the election approaching (and the time dwindling for monetary policy to take effect before the election), the elected Chancellor may have been willing to take greater inflation risks on behalf of economic growth than before.

The August *Inflation Report* was unusually frank about the consequences of the June base rate cut the Bank had opposed. Citing as evidence "lower interest rates since May, the new Treasury forecasts for taxes and public spending, and the slightly better-than-expected gross export performance in the first half of the year" (p. 45), the Bank projected that inflation would rise above 2.5 percent. Consistent with this assessment, from their August meeting on, the Governor was pressing for a rate increase, but it was only on October 30, 1996, that the Chancellor agreed to raise the base rate by a quarter point, to 6 percent. Some in the financial press speculated that the decision to raise the base rate then might be intended to avert further rate increases as the general elections, which had to be held by May 1997 at the latest, approached.[23]

This ongoing split between the agency that makes the inflation forecast and the agency that makes the policy decisions, and the bias it imparts to inflation expectations, could be characterized as the basic limitation of the largely successful inflation-targeting regime in the United Kingdom. The problem may have contributed to the decision on May 6, 1997, by the new Labour Government to grant operational independence to the Bank of England. The new Chancellor of the Exchequer, Gordon Brown, called a news conference moving up his scheduled monthly meeting with the Governor of the Bank of England; it was expected that he would announce an interest rate hike—long sought by the Bank—to deal with mounting inflation pressures (RPIX inflation was forecast to be 2.9 percent by the end of 1997). Chancellor Brown did announce a quarter-point hike in the base rate, the main monetary policy instrument, but then also made the surprise announcement that control of the base rate in pursuit of the inflation targets (as well as short-term exchange rate intervention) would now be given to the Bank of England.

One important factor in the decision to grant the Bank of England operational independence was its successful performance over time as measured against an announced clear baseline. Another factor cited by Chancellor Brown in granting independence was the increased accountability achieved through the emphasis on transparency in the inflation-targeting framework—a change that made monetary policy from an independent central bank more responsive to political oversight. When monetary policy goals and performance in meeting them are publicly stated, as they are in the U.K.'s inflation-targeting regime, the policies pursued cannot diverge from the interests of society at large for extended periods of time, yet can be insulated from short-run political considerations.

Decision-making power was vested in a newly created Monetary Policy Committee, and beginning in June, meetings of that Committee replaced the Chancellor-Governor meetings. The Committee consisted of nine members: the Governor and two Deputy Governors (one for monetary policy, one for financial matters), two other Bank Executive Directors, and four members appointed by the government (all well-known academic or financial economists). Members serve (eventually staggered) three-year renewable terms.

The elected government retained a "national interest" control over monetary policy, in essence an escape clause allowing it to overrule the Bank's interest rate decisions or pursuit of the inflation target when it deemed such action necessary. The government did not specify ahead of time any formal process for implementing the escape clause or any set of conditions under which the clause would hold.

On June 12, just prior to the first meeting of the Monetary Policy Committee, Chancellor Brown told the Committee to pursue a target of 2.5 percent for underlying inflation. The range was officially replaced with a 1 percent "threshold" on either side of the target. "Their function is to define the points at which I shall expect an explanatory letter from you [the Committee]," stated Brown. The open letter would require the Bank's explanation of why inflation has moved so far from the target, what policy actions will be taken to deal with it, when inflation is expected to be back on target, and how this meets its monetary policy objectives. The Chancellor retains the ability to tell the Bank how quickly he wishes the miss to be rectified (see Chote [1997]).

It is important to point out that the mandated response to a target miss in this framework is to provide more public explanation. The government is not precommitted to punishing the Bank for misses, say by dismissing the Governor, nor to a specified course of action. Thus, the government's control over the Bank of England is more like that exerted by the Canadian Parliament over the Bank of Canada than that imposed by the New Zealand government on its central bank through a very explicit and rule-like escape clause. As in all the cases we consider except the Bundesbank, however, the level and time horizon of the inflation target remained under the Cabinet's control—the Bank was not granted goal independence.[24]

As we noted at the start of this section, we would expect this change in framework to increase transparency of monetary policy by tying decisions to the published *Inflation Report* forecasts (and reasoning), thereby increasing accountability and decreasing interest rate uncertainty. In addition, such a move may be expected to increase the credibility of the United Kingdom's commitment to its inflation targets, because deviations from target now require the government to overrule the Bank publicly or to reset the target. Under the old regime, the government could potentially attribute deviations from the announced target to disagreements over short-run forecasts.

KEY LESSONS FROM THE
UNITED KINGDOM'S EXPERIENCE

The United Kingdom's experience has particularly interesting lessons for inflation targeting. Until May 1997, inflation targeting was conducted under severe political constraints—that is, under a system in which the govern-

ment, not the central bank, set the monetary policy instruments. As a result, it was not at all clear what motivated decisions to move (or keep steady) interest rates: was it differences in forecasts between the Chancellor and the Governor or differences in commitment to the announced inflation goals? Also unclear was the party accountable for achieving the inflation targets: was it the agency that made public forecasts (the Bank of England) or the agency that set the monetary policy instruments (the Chancellor of the Exchequer)? In addition, as we noted above, this lack of clarity led to much confusion about the degree of commitment to inflation targets and gave a strong impression that short-run political considerations were influencing monetary policy.

Despite this handicap, however, British inflation targeting has helped produce lower and more stable inflation rates. The success of inflation targeting in the United Kingdom can be attributed to the Bank of England's focus on transparency and the effective explanation of monetary policy strategy. Perhaps because for many years its position was weaker than that of the other central banks discussed here, the Bank of England led the way in producing innovative ways of communicating with the public, especially through its *Inflation Report*. Indeed, the Bank of England's achievements in communication have been emulated by many other central banks pursuing inflation targeting.

Economic Time Line: United Kingdom

Chart 1

RPIX Inflation and Targets

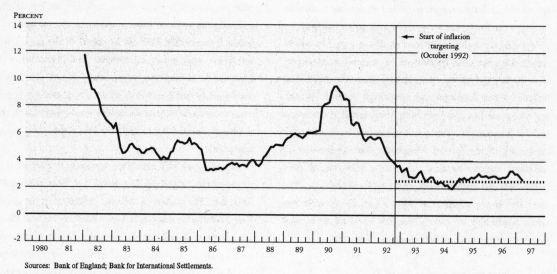

Sources: Bank of England; Bank for International Settlements.

Note: The chart shows the shift from an inflation target range of 1 to 4 percent, in effect from October 1992 to June 1995, to a point target of 2.5 percent (the midpoint of the range, marked by a dashed line).

Chart 2

Overnight and Long-Term Interest Rates

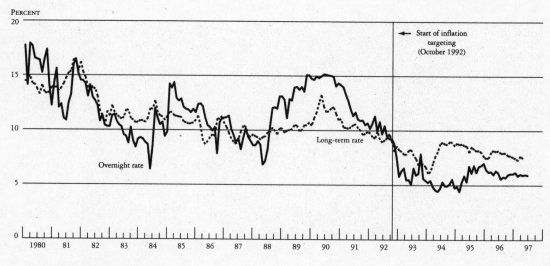

Source: Bank for International Settlements.

Chart 3

NOMINAL EFFECTIVE EXCHANGE RATE

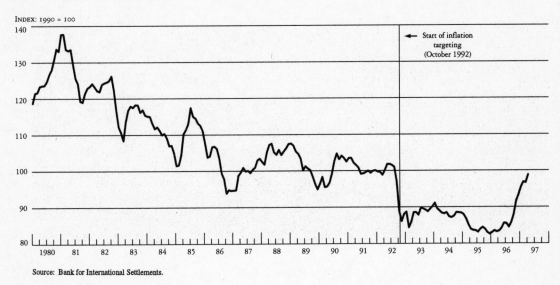

Source: Bank for International Settlements.

Chart 4

GDP GROWTH AND UNEMPLOYMENT

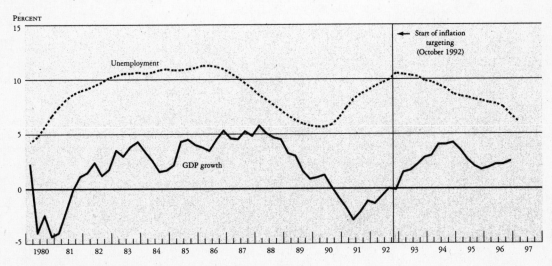

Source: Organization for Economic Cooperation and Development, *Main Economic Indicators.*

Part VII. How Successful Has Inflation Targeting Been?

An initial look suggests that inflation targeting has been a success: inflation was within or below the target range for all targeting countries, and noticeably below the countries' average inflation levels of the 1970s and 1980s. The macroeconomic baselines shown in the chart series in Parts III-VI of this study indicate that the reduced inflation levels in these countries were sustained without benefit or harm from unusual macroeconomic conditions.

In New Zealand, the disinflation during the four years prior to target adoption was accompanied by a period of sluggish GDP growth and, since 1988, rising unemployment. The continuation of the disinflation during 1990-91, amid recession in many other Organization for Economic Cooperation and Development (OECD) economies, led to recession and sharply rising unemployment. In Canada, the disinflation was achieved along with continued progress in lowering unemployment, only a brief spike in nominal interest rates, and continued positive, though slowing, growth. Similarly, in the United Kingdom, the disinflation begun two years prior to target adoption (during membership in the Exchange Rate Mechanism) continued against a background of improving growth, falling unemployment, and much lower nominal interest rates in the wake of the United Kingdom's exit from the European Monetary System.

Yet, while the reduction of inflation in these three countries represents a genuine achievement, it is not clear whether the reduction was the result of forces that had already been put in place before inflation targeting was adopted. Did the adoption of an inflation target in the countries considered here have an effect on inflation and on its interaction with real economic variables? In this section, we provide some tentative evidence on this question by undertaking a very simple forecasting exercise. (Additional evidence from a wider range of statistical investigations on a larger set of countries is found in Laubach and Posen [1997b].) We estimate a three-variable unrestricted vector autoregression (VAR) model of core inflation, GDP growth, and the central bank's overnight instrument interest rate from the second quarter of 1971 to the date of target adoption; we then allow the system to run forward five years from the time of target adoption, plugging in the model's forecast values as lagged values.[1]

This exercise is meant to give a quantitative impression of whether the interaction between inflation and short-term interest rates exhibits a pattern of behavior after the adoption of the inflation target that differs markedly from the pattern before.[2] The unconditional forecast of each variable represents the way we would expect the system to behave in the absence of shocks from the situation at the time of target adoption. The comparison between what actually happened to these variables and their unconditional forecast is reasonable for the early 1990s, given the absence of major supply and demand shocks since adoption for the three inflation targeters we examine.[3]

In the three countries adopting inflation targets, disinflation through tighter monetary policy had largely been completed by the time the target was adopted, allowing interest rates to come down. (The year or so of further disinflation appears to be attributable to prior monetary policy moves, given policy lags.) This sequence of events is consistent with our finding in the case studies that countries adopted targets when they wished to lock in inflation expectations at a low level after a disinflation. The key question is whether upward blips in inflation do or do not lead to persistent rises—holding output and inflation constant—as they would have in a system estimated under the prior regime.

Charts 1-4 (pp. 89-92) plot the results of these simulations against the actual path of the variables over the period for each of the three inflation-targeting countries plus Germany. As might be expected, the simulations over time flatten out toward their sample means or a slight trend (given the absence of shocks imposed by the unconditionality of the simulation). For all three inflation targeters, the actual inflation rate comes in consistently below what would have been expected and exhibits something of a downward trend as opposed to the simulation's slight upward tendency. Complementarily, for all three targeters, the actual interest rate used as the monetary policy instrument remains well below the simulation's forecast throughout the period. Output appears to be largely undisturbed by the adoption of targeting, averaging around the projected path in all three countries. In general, inflation and nominal short-term interest rates seem to have declined since target adoption without any major effect on output.

These results can be interpreted as consistent with a greater direct response of inflation to monetary policy with fewer output effects along the way, given the movement of interest rates at or below those forecast on average in the three targeters. Alternatively, these results can be an indication that in the targeting countries, disinflation through tighter monetary policy had begun and been largely completed by the time that targeting began, but that inflation did not bounce back up afterward as expected.[4]

By contrast, the simulations for Germany clearly reflect the effects of monetary unification, with both inflation and the monetary policy instrument exceeding their projections and returning to them only in early 1994. GDP growth initially exceeded the projection as a result of the expansion in aggregate demand, until in 1992 and 1993 the effects of the increasingly restrictive monetary policy—as seen in interest rates well above those forecast into the second half of 1994—forced output growth below its projected trend. We interpret the return over time of inflation and the monetary policy instrument to their projected levels after a surprise demand shock of great magnitude as a characteristic of a successful targeting regime.

Our assessment of the effectiveness of inflation targeting in New Zealand, Canada, and the United Kingdom is on the whole positive. In all three countries, the adoption of targets was followed by the movement of inflation into, and the maintenance of inflation within, the announced target range. In the time since the adoption of inflation targets, our unconditional forecasts indicate that inflation and nominal interest rates have remained low in all three countries relative to the amount of output growth seen (which itself approximates the level forecast). This set of results is consistent with the interpretation that inflation does not appear to rise with business cycle expansions as it had in the past. Laubach and Posen (1997b) provide further support for this interpretation, presenting evidence from private sector forecasts and interest rate differentials that medium- and long-run inflation expectations in New Zealand, Canada, and the United Kingdom lie within these countries' target ranges.

Chart 1

DYNAMIC SIMULATIONS: GERMANY

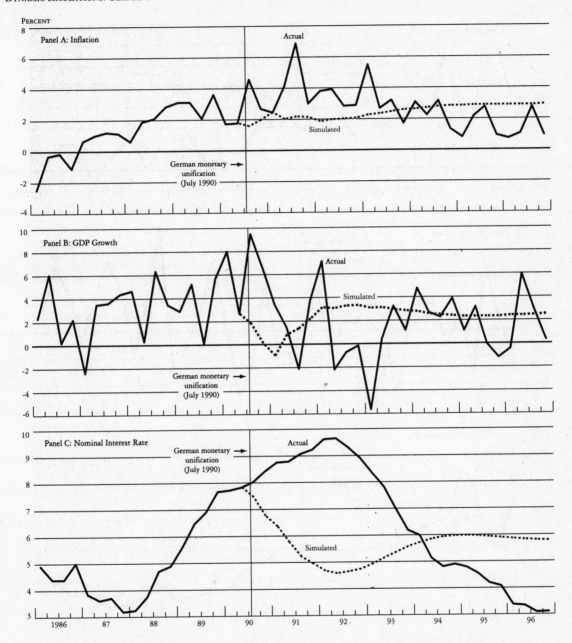

PERCENT

Panel A: Inflation

Actual

Simulated

German monetary →
unification
(July 1990)

Panel B: GDP Growth

Actual

Simulated

German monetary →
unification
(July 1990)

Panel C: Nominal Interest Rate

German monetary →
unification
(July 1990)

Actual

Simulated

1986 87 88 89 90 91 92 93 94 95 96

Sources: Authors' calculations; Bank for International Settlements; Organization for Economic Cooperation and Development, *Main Economic Indicators*.

Notes: The chart depicts the results of a dynamic simulation of inflation, GDP growth, and the nominal interest rate based on an unrestricted vector autoregression (VAR) of quarterly observations of these three variables from the second quarter of 1971 up to the time of German monetary unification. The solid line represents the actual values of the variables, and the dashed line represents the unconstrained forecast of the variables made from unification forward using the VAR coefficients. The forecasts show the path the variables would have taken in the absence of German monetary unification and other unforeseen shocks. In panel C, the nominal interest rate used is the central bank's instrument interest rate.

Chart 2

DYNAMIC SIMULATIONS: NEW ZEALAND

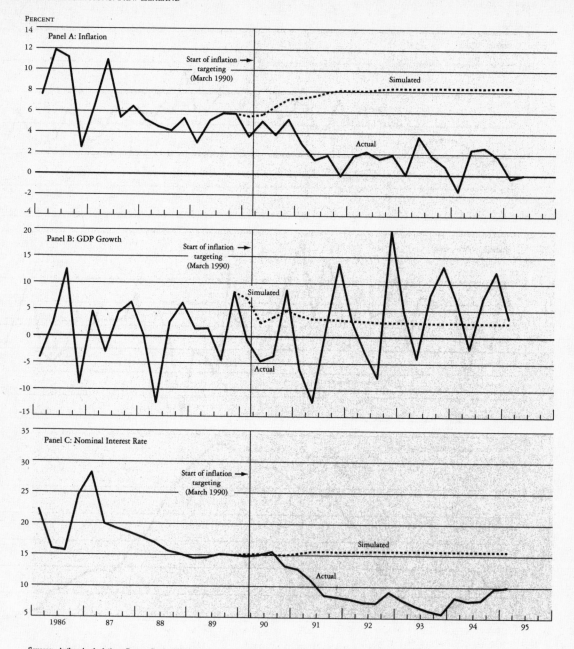

Sources: Authors' calculations; Reserve Bank of New Zealand; International Monetary Fund, International Financial Statistics.

Notes: The chart depicts the results of a dynamic simulation of inflation, GDP growth, and the nominal interest rate based on an unrestricted vector autoregression (VAR) of quarterly observations of these three variables from the second quarter of 1971 up to the time of inflation target adoption. The solid line represents the actual values of the variables, and the dashed line represents the unconstrained forecast of the variables made from adoption forward using the VAR coefficients. The forecasts show the path the variables would have taken in the absence of inflation targeting and other unforeseen shocks. In panel C, the nominal interest rate used is the New Zealand ninety-day bank bill rate.

Chart 3

DYNAMIC SIMULATIONS: CANADA

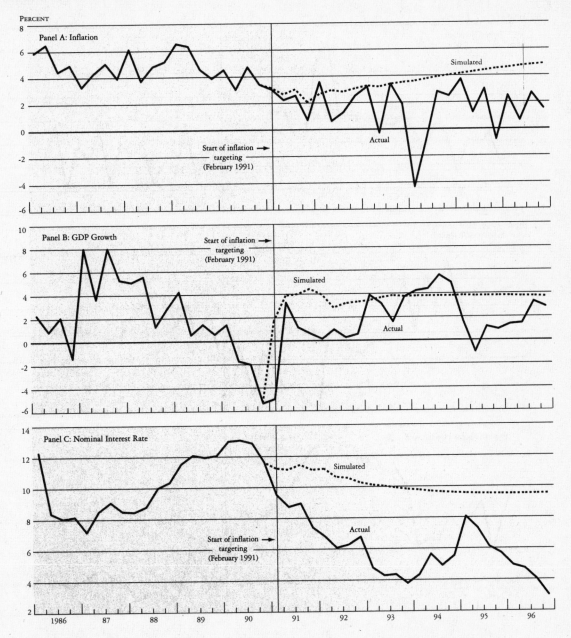

PERCENT

Panel A: Inflation

Simulated

Actual

Start of inflation →
targeting
(February 1991)

Panel B: GDP Growth

Start of inflation →
targeting
(February 1991)

Simulated

Actual

Panel C: Nominal Interest Rate

Simulated

Actual

Start of inflation →
targeting
(February 1991)

1986   87   88   89   90   91   92   93   94   95   96

Sources: Authors' calculations; Bank for International Settlements; Organization for Economic Cooperation and Development, *Main Economic Indicators*.

Notes: The chart depicts the results of a dynamic simulation of inflation, GDP growth, and the nominal interest rate based on an unrestricted vector autoregression (VAR) of quarterly observations of these three variables from the second quarter of 1971 up to the time of inflation target adoption. The solid line represents the actual values of the variables, and the dashed line represents the unconstrained forecast of the variables made from adoption forward using the VAR coefficients. The forecasts show the path the variables would have taken in the absence of inflation targeting and other unforeseen shocks. In panel C, the nominal interest rate used is the central bank's instrument interest rate.

Chart 4

DYNAMIC SIMULATIONS: UNITED KINGDOM

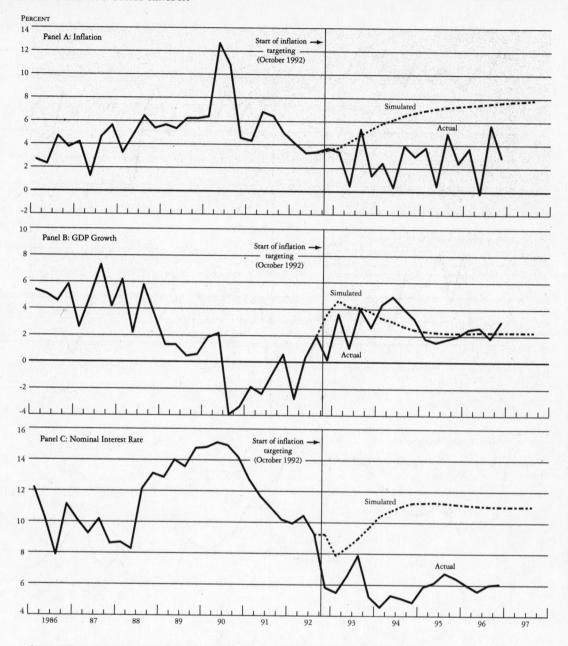

Sources: Authors' calculations; Bank for International Settlements; Organization for Economic Cooperation and Development, *Main Economic Indicators.*

Notes: The chart depicts the results of a dynamic simulation of inflation, GDP growth, and the nominal interest rate based on an unrestricted vector autoregression (VAR) of quarterly observations of these three variables from the second quarter of 1971 up to the time of inflation target adoption. The solid line represents the actual values of the variables, and the dashed line represents the unconstrained forecast of the variables made from adoption forward using the VAR coefficients. The forecasts show the path the variables would have taken in the absence of inflation targeting and other unforeseen shocks. In panel C, the nominal interest rate used is the central bank's instrument interest rate.

Part VIII. Conclusions: What Have We Learned?

Our case studies indicate that both the adoption of inflation targets and the design choices for that framework have made a difference in the operation of monetary policy. The design choices of the targeting countries have tended to converge over time with regard to the operational design questions posed in Part II, suggesting that a consensus is emerging on best practice in the operation of an inflation-targeting regime. Where the design choices have differed, however, the experiences in the countries examined provide some insight about what has resulted from the different choices. In general, the public announcement of numerical targets for inflation has been very effective in balancing the needs for transparency and flexibility in monetary policy.

The areas of operational design that show a convergence of practice include the use of inflation as the target variable. Despite all the rhetoric associated with the pursuit of price stability, all the targeting countries examined here have chosen an inflation target—ranging from 0 to 4 percent annual inflation—rather than a price-level target. This choice reflects concerns that a price-level target may require deflation when prices overshoot the target, an outcome that could entail far higher costs in output losses than are acceptable. Reversals of past target misses, which would be required by a price-level target, do not appear to be necessary for the maintenance of low inflation. Relatedly, targeting countries that have chosen target values for inflation greater than zero make the possibility of deflations less likely. It is important to emphasize that maintaining an inflation target at a level even somewhat greater than zero for an extended period, as the Bundesbank has done, does not appear to lead to instability in inflation expectations or diminished central bank credibility. Even with a positive inflation target, admission of occasional errors does not appear to be damaging.

These design choices are also consistent with building a high degree of flexibility into the inflation-targeting regimes in all the countries studied here, in which central bankers do demonstrate concern about real output growth and fluctuations. This is seen particularly in the gradualism all targeting countries have exercised when disinflating, as well as in the treatment by some countries of the inflation target's (implicit or explicit) floor on price movements as a stabilizing factor. While the targeting countries differ in the degree to which they emphasize particular indicators of inflation in their decision making, all rely on an inclusive information framework untied to specific intermediate target variables. All of these design choices support the contention in Bernanke and Mishkin (1997) that inflation targeting should be seen as a framework rather than a rule.

In addition, all of the targeting countries allow for deviations from their targets in response to supply shocks. Usually, the central bank will take action at its own discretion, when such a response is not already built into the target definition, and then explain its actions. Only in New Zealand has an explicit escape clause been invoked to justify such actions, although the Reserve Bank of New Zealand has also engaged in the more discretionary forms of response. Actual inflation targets have been moved over time by all targeting countries, whether up—as in the case of Germany after the 1979 oil shock or New Zealand after the 1996 election—or down—as in all countries considered as disinflations proceeded. As long as target movements are announced sufficiently far in advance, there is no sense that the target is being moved to meet the short-run outcome; target movements are perceived as adaptations to economic conditions. The key to the exercise of discretion in a disciplined manner has been the central banks' ability to convey to the public the distinction between movements in trend inflation and onetime events.

The second main area in which targeting regimes have converged relates to their stress on transparency and communication. The central banks in targeting countries communicate by responding to elected officials' mandated as well as informal inquiries. Even more important, the central banks keep the public informed about their policies and performance by making frequent speeches on the strategy of monetary policy, as in the Bank of Canada Governing Council's concerted public outreach campaign, and by periodically issuing lay-oriented publications, such as the Bank of England's *Inflation Report*. Both of these efforts are designed to explain clearly to the public the goals of monetary policy, the long-run implications of current policy, and the strategies for achieving inflation targets. Even the fully independent Bundesbank, which enjoys strong public support, has always made great efforts along these lines.

Indeed, the intensive efforts by the central banks we study here to improve communication have been crucial to the success of the targeting regimes. Increased transparency and communication make explicit the central bank's policy intentions in a way that improves private sector planning, enhances the possibility of sensible public debate about what a central bank can and cannot achieve, and clarifies the responsibility of both the central bank and the politicians for the performance of monetary policy with respect to inflation goals.

Another feature of all the targeting regimes discussed here is the increased accountability of the central bank. This feature is most evident in the case of New Zealand, where the Reserve Bank is accountable not only to the general public, but also (and even more directly) to the elected government, which can insist on the dismissal of the Governor if the inflation targets are breached. In the other targeting countries, the accountability of the central bank to the government is less formalized, but because of the increased transparency of the targeting regime, the central

bank is still highly accountable to the general public and the political process.

As seen in the cases of Canada and the United Kingdom, as well as in the Bundesbank's long experience, even where a rigid format of performance evaluation and punishment is not present, successful performance over time against an announced clear baseline can build public support for a central bank's independence and its policies. Inflation targeting may thus be seen as consistent with an appropriate role for a central bank in a democratic society: though inflation performance may improve by insulating a central bank from short-term political pressures on interest rate decisions, a central bank can only sustain such performance by remaining highly accountable to the political process over the medium term for achieving appropriate, stated goals. When monetary policy goals and performance in meeting them are publicly stated, they cannot diverge from the interests of society at large for extended periods of time.

Another design choice common to the inflation-targeting countries is the decision to formally adopt the new regime only after achieving some success in lowering inflation from high levels. This reflects a tactical decision that it is important to have a high likelihood of success in meeting the initial inflation targets in order to gain credibility for the inflation-targeting regime. It also reflects the reality that credibility gains in the form of changes in the output-inflation trade-off or other economic structures will not occur immediately. Inflation targeting has been successfully used to lock in the benefits of previous disinflations in the face of imminent onetime shocks, as we saw in the United Kingdom's exit from the European Exchange Rate Mechanism and Canada's 1991 fiscal developments.

Although there are many similarities among the design choices of the targeting countries studied here, there are also some important differences. For example, the targeting countries differ on the precise *measure* of inflation that should be used for the target. Some countries use the headline consumer price index (CPI) as the price index in the inflation target because it is readily understood by the public, while others exclude items from the CPI index to allow for monetary policy accommodation of first-round effects of temporary supply shocks. In the cases of Germany, Canada, and the United Kingdom, the emphasis has been on simple target definitions, accompanied by potentially complicated explanations of deviations from target, while in New Zealand the reverse course has been pursued (although the long-run goal remains underlying inflation). The primary danger for any target series, however defined, is to sacrifice transparency for policy flexibility. So long as a target series is neither adjusted too frequently nor set too far from headline inflation, so that the definition remains clear in the mind of the public, the exact choice of series is not that critical.

Indeed, this balancing of transparency and flexibility relates to the manner of producing the measured inflation series as well as to the definition per se. To permit flexibility in its inflation-targeting regime, New Zealand has allowed the agency that is accountable for meeting the targets (the Reserve Bank) to measure and make adjustments to the target variable as well. In contrast, the other countries studied separate the agency responsible for meeting the targets from the agency that measures the target variable. Although allowing the central bank to measure and adjust the target variable has distinct advantages in terms of increased flexibility, it has the undesirable effect of decreasing transparency, which can weaken the effectiveness of the inflation-targeting regime.

Another major difference in the design of inflation-targeting regimes is that some countries have a target range for inflation while others, such as the United Kingdom, now have a point target. The apparent advantage of a range is that it gives the targeting regime more explicit flexibility and conveys to the public the message that control of inflation is imperfect. Nevertheless, as we have seen in countries targeting an inflation range, and as we know from the similar experience of exchange rate targeting, the bands tend to take on a life of their own, encouraging central banks, politicians, and the public to focus too much on the exact edges of the range rather than on deviations from the midpoint of the range. Furthermore, because a high degree of uncertainty is associated with inflation forecasts, it is very likely that even with entirely appropriate monetary policy, the inflation rate may fall outside the target range. This control problem can then lead to a loss of credibility for the inflation-targeting regime.

In addition, firm bands can also lead to an instrument-instability problem, particularly if the time horizon for assessing whether the target has been met is short—say on the order of a year. This problem occurs when efforts to keep the targeted variable within a specified range cause policy instruments, such as short-term interest rates or the exchange rate, to undergo undesirably large movements. The control and instrument-instability problems have been comparatively more difficult in the case of New Zealand.

One solution to these problems is to widen the target range, as New Zealand did in October 1996. However, if the range is made wide enough to reduce the instrument-instability and control problems significantly, the targeting regime may lose credibility. This would be particularly true if the public focuses on the edges of the range rather than the midpoint, with an upper limit that might then be intolerably high. The act of widening the range (as distinct from moving the target level in accord with events) might be seen as a weakening of resolve in and of itself.

Another solution is to use a point target rather than a range, as the United Kingdom decided to do in 1995 and as the Bundesbank has done for inflation since 1975. To avoid control and instrument-instability problems with a point target, however, it is imperative that the central bank communicate clearly to the public that a great deal of uncertainty exists around the point target. This communication imposes a greater burden on the power and persuasiveness of the central bank's explanations for deviations from target than exists with a range. At the same time, the central bank's actual flexibility to cope with target misses without damage to credibility is greater as long as the explanations are believed. With a point target, success is not measured by hitting the target exactly, but rather by how consistently the central bank gets close to the target over a medium term.

The analysis in this paper suggests that targeting inflation—whether directly, as in New Zealand, Canada, and the United Kingdom, or as the basis for a monetary targeting regime, as in Germany—can be a useful strategy for the conduct of monetary policy. Since the defining feature of the monetary frameworks in all four countries is the publicly announced numerical target for medium-term inflation, we do not draw as great a distinction between these two types of targeting regimes in operation as many do in theory. Transparency and flexibility, properly balanced in operational design, appear to create a sound foundation for a monetary strategy in pursuit of price stability, without requiring the imposition of unnecessary rule-like constraints on policy.

That said, as our case studies suggest, inflation targeting is no panacea: it does not enable countries to eliminate inflation from their systems without cost, and anti-inflation credibility is not achieved immediately upon the adoption of an inflation target. Indeed, the evidence suggests that the only way for central banks to gain credibility is the hard way: they have to earn it.

Still, we have seen that inflation targeting has been highly successful in helping countries such as New Zealand, Canada, and the United Kingdom to maintain low inflation rates, something that they have not always been able to do in the past. Furthermore, inflation targeting has not required the central banks to abandon their concerns about other economic outcomes, such as the level of the exchange rate or the rate of economic growth, in order to achieve low inflation rates. Indeed, there is no evidence that inflation targeting has produced undesirable effects on the real economy in the long run; instead, it has likely had the effect of improving the climate for economic growth. Given inflation targeting's other benefits for the operation of monetary policy—it increases transparency and communication, accountability, and the institutional commitment to low inflation—it is a monetary policy strategy that deserves further study and consideration.

ENDNOTES

INTRODUCTION

1. See a companion piece to this study, Bernanke and Mishkin (1997), for a more theoretical discussion of the rationale for inflation targeting. In particular, the authors stress that inflation targeting should be seen not as a rule, but as a framework that has substantial flexibility.

PART I. THE RATIONALE FOR INFLATION TARGETING

1. "I believe that the potentiality of monetary policy in offsetting other forces making for instability is far more limited than is commonly believed. We simply do not know enough to be able to recognize minor disturbances when they occur or to be able to predict either what their effects will be with any precision or what monetary policy is required to offset their effects. We do not know enough to be able to achieve stated objectives by delicate, or even fairly coarse, changes in the mix of monetary and fiscal policy" (Friedman 1968, p. 14).

2. This argument is made in the leading macroeconomics and money and banking textbooks. For examples, see the discussion in Dornbusch and Fischer (1994, p. 437), Hall and Taylor (1993, pp. 440-1), Mankiw (1994, p. 323), and Mishkin (1994, pp. 701-4).

3. This view is accepted in the leading macroeconomics and monetary economics textbooks. For examples, see Abel and Bernanke (1995, pp. 458-9), Barro (1993, p. 497), Hall and Taylor (1993, p. 222), Mankiw (1994, p. 479), and Mishkin (1994, pp. 651-4).

4. This argument was developed in papers by Kydland and Prescott (1977), Calvo (1978), and Barro and Gordon (1983).

5. Briault (1995) gives a good summary of these effects.

6. Sarel (1996), for example, presents a strong argument that the growth costs of inflation are nonlinear and rise significantly when inflation exceeds 8 percent annually.

7. See Judson and Orphanides (1996). Hess and Morris (1996) also disentangle the relationship between inflation variability and the inflation level for low-inflation countries.

8. For central bankers' views, see Crow (1988), Leigh-Pemberton (1992), and McDonough (1996a); for academics' views, see Fischer (1994) and Goodhart and Viñals (1995).

There is also a literature suggesting that lower inflation will not only produce a higher level of output but also cause higher rates of economic growth, thereby providing a further reason for pursuing the goal of price stability. For example, see Fisher (1981, 1991, 1993), Bruno and Easterly (1995), and Barro (1995).

9. However, as pointed out in Bernanke and Mishkin (1997), the provisions for short-run stabilization objectives in inflation-targeting regimes suggest that, in practice, inflation targeting may not be very different from nominal GDP targeting.

PART III. GERMAN MONETARY TARGETING: A PRECURSOR TO INFLATION TARGETING

1. Laubach and Posen (1997a) provides a more detailed analysis of the German case as well as a comparison with the Swiss monetary targeting regime and address many of the same themes.

2. While this belief may indeed be consistent with later academic arguments that there is an inflationary bias to monetary policy (for example, because of time inconsistency) requiring a central bank to tie its hands, it is important to note that Germany's adoption of monetary targeting precedes these arguments by several years. Some later observers have argued that the Germans were broadly distrustful of monetary discretion, but this interpretation should not be exaggerated through contemporary mindset. To most observers, that issue had already been addressed by the granting of independence to the Bundesbank in 1957, the distrust being the *politicization* of monetary policy.

3. The announcement was reprinted in Deutsche Bundesbank (1974b, December, p. 8).

4. The central bank money stock is defined as currency in circulation plus sight deposits, time deposits with maturity under four years, and savings deposits and savings bonds with maturity under four years, the latter three weighted at their required reserve ratios as of January 1974. The Bundesbank's rationale for this choice of intermediate target variable will be discussed in the next section.

5. Neumann (1996) and Clarida and Gertler (1997) argue both points, that the Bundesbank has multiple goals and that it does not strictly target money. Von Hagen (1995) and Bernanke and Mihov (1997) focus on the latter point, while Friedman (1995) discusses why the Bundesbank might not want to look at M3.

6. The weights are 16.6 percent, 12.4 percent, and 8.2 percent, respectively.

7. See, for example, Deutsche Bundesbank (1981a, "Recalculation of the Production Potential of the Federal Republic of Germany").

8. The vast variety and depth of information provided by the Bundesbank in its *Monthly Report* and *Annual Report* would appear to be evidence that a wide range of information variables, far beyond M3,

Note 8 (continued)

velocity, and potential GDP, play a role in Bundesbank decision making (the work involved in producing the data and analysis makes it unlikely that it is merely a smokescreen or a public service). Nevertheless, monetary policy moves are always justified with reference to M3 and/or inflation developments, rather than with these other types of data.

9. The Bundesbank describes the *Annual Report* as "a detailed presentation of economic trends, including the most recent developments, together with comments on current monetary and general economic problems."

10. Actually, it was the third year of four in a row where the 8.0 percent CBM monetary growth point target was exceeded by at least a percentage point (see Bernanke and Mishkin [1992, p. 201, Table 4]).

11. Two more technical developments also suggested the switch from CBM to M3 targets. The first was that minimum reserve requirements had changed substantially since 1974, so that CBM, computed on the basis of 1974 ratios, corresponded less and less to the monetary base and thus to "the extent to which the central bank has provided funds for the banks' money creation." The second development was the increasing need to include new components, such as Euro-deposits held by domestic nonbanks, in some broadly defined money stock for control purposes. Since these components had never been subject to minimum reserve requirements, the weight at which they should enter CBM was not clear, a problem that does not exist for some extended definition of M3.

12. "While officially the question of the correct exchange rate was still under discussion, the German Chancellor announced his decision on the exchange rate without informing Bundesbank President Karl-Otto Pöhl, although they had met only a few hours before" (Hefeker 1994, p. 383). See Marsh (1992) for a longer historical description. For most east German citizens, personal assets were converted at the rate of 1 to 1. However, for larger holdings, a declining rate of exchange was employed.

13. Since the achievement in the mid-1980s of effective price stability in Germany, the Bundesbank has spoken of "normative price increases" rather than "unavoidable inflation" in response to the high inflation of the 1970s and early 1980s (we are grateful to Otmar Issing for emphasizing this shift to us). This change in language could be interpreted as a sign that the Bundesbank expresses greater confidence in its ability to achieve its ultimately desired inflation goal.

14. For two recent examples of this repeated argument, see Issing (1995b) and Schmid (1996).

PART IV. NEW ZEALAND

1. Before the passage of the Reserve Bank of New Zealand Act of 1989, the Reserve Bank was ranked as low in independence. See Alesina and Summers (1993).

2. "The role of monetary policy under [the new government's] approach is aimed in the medium term at achieving suitably moderate and steady rates of growth in the major monetary aggregates. This is directed ultimately at the inflation rate, as control over the monetary aggregates is seen as a prerequisite for a lower, more stable rate of inflation" (Reserve Bank of New Zealand 1985b, p. 513).

3. The problem of the treatment of housing costs was addressed at the beginning of 1994, when the weight of existing dwellings in the CPI was largely replaced by including the cost of construction of new houses. Similar problems in the treatment of housing costs were a feature of the CPI in the United States before 1983.

4. This is not simply a matter of who guards the guardian, serious though that may be. "Because the Reserve Bank's estimate of underlying inflation relies on judgment in its construction, its validity cannot be directly verified [by outside observers]. In addition, there is room for disagreement concerning the proper model to be used in estimating the impact of one-time shocks" (Walsh 1995). The Reserve Bank itself has made note of this potential conflict of interest and its possible effect on credibility in articles in the *Reserve Bank of New Zealand Bulletin*.

5. Strictly speaking, the first PTA only allowed for, or required renegotiation of, the Agreement, while the second and third PTAs required such a response to shocks.

6. We are grateful to Governor Brash for clarifying this point. The exclusion of the effects of taxes imposed by local authorities proved impractical given the difficulties of identifying policy changes at that level. The effect, however, remained potentially quite large, with the movement toward "user-pays pricing" of services provided by the public sector as part of the broader reforms.

7. Some bank documents, however, have made the contradictory claim that the move to targeting and central bank independence would be expected to have an effect on the potential costs of disinflation. For example, "in order to improve the prospects of monetary policy to remain—and be seen to remain—on the track to low inflation, and thereby help reduce the costs of disinflation, attention turned to possible institutional arrangements which would improve monetary policy credibility" (Lloyd 1992, p. 208). See Posen (1995), Hutchison and Walsh (1996), and Laubach and Posen (1997b) for econometric assessments of this effect.

8. Again, this may be contrasted to the Bundesbank's framework, which does not address the short-run real effects of monetary policy in public statements but keeps all responsibility for the timing and duration of disinflation with the Bundesbank.

9. The article cited here, while signed by Lloyd, not only appeared in the *Reserve Bank of New Zealand Bulletin* under the authoritative title "The New Zealand Approach to Central Bank Autonomy," but parts of it also appeared verbatim in other statements by Reserve Bank of New Zealand officials given in 1992 and 1993, so it is reasonable to treat this statement as representative of the Bank's view.

10. With regard to financial stability, inflation targeting has an important advantage over an exchange rate peg because under an inflation target, the central bank has the ability to act as a lender of last resort. This option is not as available with a fixed exchange rate regime, as the Argentinean experience in 1995 demonstrates (see, for example, Mishkin [1997]).

11. A similar point about the gap between the perception and the operational reality of monetary targeting in Germany was made in the case study in Part III.

12. For brevity, references in this section are given by the month and year of the *Monetary Policy Statement*.

13. See, for example, *New Zealand Herald* (1990a).

14. See *New Zealand Herald* (1990b). Interestingly, after losing power, the Labour Party, which instituted the inflation targets (and the economic reforms, more generally) after taking office in 1984, announced its opposition to the inflation target remaining at a narrow 2 percent band, although it continued to be adamant that the center of the target range should remain at 1 percent.

15. In March 1997, the Bank discussed moving to a more directly controlled instrument rate, but in June the Bank announced that a directly controlled interest rate would in fact not be adopted.

16. See, for example, Reuters Financial Service (1991).

17. Until December 1993, the Bank's inflation forecasts assumed that the exchange rate would remain constant at the level present at the time of the forecast. The vindication of the statement above over the preceding two years led the Bank in June 1994 to assume from that point on an annual appreciation equal to the difference between the trade-weighted inflation forecasts for New Zealand's main trading partners and the midpoint of the 0 to 2 percent target range from June 1994.

18. See, for example, Louisson (1994).

19. We are grateful to Governor Brash for his discussion of these developments.

20. Proportional representation was approved in a nationwide referendum. It was largely interpreted as a means for the public to put a brake on activist programs by the government—be they of the right or left reform persuasion—for under majoritarian parliaments, New Zealand had seen major shifts (such as Labour's "Rogernomics" reforms after 1984), whereas coalition governments would be less likely to accomplish this. The effects of multiple parties on inflation rates and fiscal policy (usually held to increase the former and loosen the latter in the economics literature) do not seem to have entered the discussions.

PART V. CANADA

1. To cite two examples of expectational sluggishness: "There is no doubt that Canadian markets are not at all supportive of inflationary actions nowadays. But it does take time for such reality to have an impact on market behavior, and on the costs and prices that flow from this behavior" (Crow 1991b, p. 13); "the lags in the response of the Canadian rate of inflation to changes in monetary policy have traditionally been long, both as a result of institutional characteristics . . . and expectational sluggishness" (Freedman 1994a, p. 21). Moreover, Longworth and Freedman (1995) explain how backward-looking expectations play a significant role in the current Bank of Canada forecasting model.

2. See similar statements in Jenkins (1990), Bank of Canada (1991c), and Freedman (1994a).

3. The example of New Zealand was probably not yet well established, and it is not acknowledged in public statements by senior Bank officials until Freedman (1994a).

4. Thiessen (1994a, p. 86) makes an almost identical statement of these two points.

5. "Over longer periods of time, the measures of inflation based on the total CPI and the core CPI tend to follow similar paths. In the event of persistent differences between the trends of the two measures, the Bank would adjust its desired path for core CPI inflation so that total CPI inflation would come within the target range" (Bank of Canada 1996, November, p. 4).

6. "Accommodating the initial effect on the price level of a tax change but not any ongoing inflation effects was the approach set out with the February 1991 inflation-reduction targets, and restated in the December

Note 6 (continued)

1993 agreement [extending the target framework]" (Thiessen 1994a, p. 82). Of course, unlike the assessment of differences between core and headline CPI, the assessment of the size of a tax increase's initial as opposed to pass-through effect on prices depends on an analyst's assumptions. The Bank does publish its own calculations of the price effects of tax changes.

7. "It is important to stress that the objective continues to be the control of inflation as defined by the total consumer price index" (Thiessen 1996d, p. 4).

8. "The targets continue to be expressed as a range or a band rather than a specific inflation rate because it is impossible to control inflation precisely" (Thiessen 1994a, p. 86).

9. "Other sources of unexpected price increases, which are typically less significant than the three singled out for special attention, will be handled within the one percent band around the targets for reducing inflation" (Bank of Canada 1991c, p. 4).

10. This may be due to the fact that more than any other inflation-targeting country, Canada has had to cope with headline inflation falling below the target or reaching the target ahead of schedule and, perhaps as a result, with greater public criticism of the targets as harmful to the real economy. These challenges are discussed in the next section.

11. See Thiessen (1994a, p. 89) and Freedman (1994a, p. 20) for examples.

12. This statement is representative of the Bank's position. See also, for example, Bank of Canada (1995, May), which states: "The ultimate objective of Canadian monetary policy is to promote good overall economic performance. Monetary policy can contribute to this goal by preserving confidence in the value of money through price stability. In other words, price stability is a means to an end, not an end in itself."

13. This interpretation of short-run flexibility was raised in a different context in Bernanke and Mishkin (1992). In a more recent example, in the Bank of Canada's *Annual Report, 1994*, the Bank states that "in late 1994 and early 1995, the persistent weakness of the dollar began to undermine confidence in the currency, and the Bank of Canada took actions to calm and stabilize financial markets" (p. 7), while the *Annual Report, 1996* lists "promoting the safety and soundness of Canada's financial system" (p. 4) as the second part of its section "Our Commitment to Canadians." In short, the Bank found no inherent conflict between seeking within limits either the goal of financial stability or the goal of limiting real economic swings (as seen in the

gradual convergence discussed above) and the pursuit of price stability over the long run. In this characteristic, it is similar to all central banks we studied, though perhaps more open about it.

14. Real—that is, inflation-indexed return—bonds have been issued in Canada since 1991 following the example of the United Kingdom. One motive cited for the creation of these real bonds was precisely to obtain a measure of inflation expectations. As the Bank of Canada itself has pointed out, however, the market for real bonds to date has been relatively small and illiquid. In addition, it has only a short history, which makes direct measurement of the implicit inflation expectations difficult.

15. This idea has been picked up since by a number of other countries and several private sector forecasting groups as a compact means of expressing the relative tightness of monetary policy in open economies.

16. For a more complete discussion of the MCI, see Freedman (1994b).

17. Freedman (1995, p. 30) offers the opinion that "it may well be that their [*Monetary Policy Report*'s] most important contribution will be to signal prospective inflationary pressure and the need for timely policy action, at a time when actual rates of inflation (which are of course a lagging indicator) are still relatively subdued." This scenario is premised on Canada starting from a situation of "relatively subdued" inflation pressures, which was the case by 1995.

18. Citing New Zealand, the United Kingdom, and Sweden, Freedman (1995, pp. 29-30) notes, "These reports, which have both backward-looking and forward-looking perspectives, have received considerable attention and careful scrutiny by the press, the financial markets, and parliamentary committees." See also Thiessen (1995d, p. 56), who states: "This report will provide an account of our stewardship of monetary policy and will be useful for those who want to know more about monetary policy for their own decision-making."

19. This move may have seemed necessary after the October 1993 election was fought in part over the Bank's monetary policy, and Crow eventually decided not to be considered for a second term. The newly elected Liberal Government chose to extend rather than to replace the inflation targets. This event demonstrates how inflation-targeting frameworks can differ or change along the axis of accountability independently of their stated inflation goals and monetary policy procedures (which may remain the same).

20. According to Cukierman's (1992) legal index of central bank independence, the Bank of Canada ranks, with the Danish central bank, just below the Federal Reserve in independence.

21. Laidler and Robson (1993, Chap. 9) provide an extensive discussion of the Bank of Canada's practical independence and its limits up through 1992.

22. In this regard, Canada's framework is even more similar to that of Switzerland—a country that, like Canada, has a small, open economy. See Laubach and Posen (1997a).

23. *Creating Opportunity: The Liberal Plan for Canada,* cited in Crane (1993).

24. The targets were intended to define the path implied by the various actual inflation targets at eighteen-month intervals of 3 percent by year-end 1992, 2.5 percent by mid-1994, and 2 percent by year-end 1995.

25. For example, "'the government is betting on its own inflation targets,' said Toronto-Dominion Bank chief economist Doug Peters, referring to Canada's target of 2 percent inflation in 1995" (Szep 1991).

26. See, for example, Ip (1991).

27. The committee's formal title was the Standing Committee on Finance, Subcommittee on the Bank of Canada, of the House of Commons, but it was called the Manley Committee after its chairman, John Manley. See its report, *The Mandate and Governance of the Bank of Canada,* February 1992.

28. It should be noted that, for all the attention central banks' written charters and legal mandates attract, there are only a few central banks that have dedicated price stability mandates. Not only have many inflation targeters—such as Canada, Sweden, Australia, and the United Kingdom—adopted largely successful inflation-targeting regimes without revision of their legal mission, but the Bundesbank is the only one of the three independent central banks with a long-standing successful inflation record (the Swiss National Bank and the U.S. Federal Reserve are the others) that has had such a clearly limited legal mandate.

29. The Liberal Party's campaign platform, *Creating Opportunity: The Liberal Plan for Canada*, included the statements: "Liberals believe that economic policies must not merely attack an individual problem in isolation from its costs in other areas. . . . The Conservatives' single-minded fight against inflation resulted in deep recession, three years without growth, declining incomes, skyrocketing unemployment, a crisis in international payments, and the highest combined set of government deficits in our history." See Crane (1993).

30. For a sample of private sector reactions, see Marotte (1993).

31. For press coverage of Freedman's speech, see, among others, Ip (1993).

32. During the period of an announced downward path for inflation, the emphasis in the Bank of Canada's discussion was on the midpoint, whereas once the range of 1 to 3 percent was reached, the emphasis shifted to the bands. We are grateful to Charles Freedman for discussion of this point.

33. Some press observers characterized the contemporaneous developments in transparency undertaken by the Bank as reflecting a desire to make the Bank seem more generally accountable rather than identified with a particular individual. See, for example, Vardy (1993) and McGillivray (1994).

34. The Bank had explained beforehand that it expected only a temporary blip in inflation in 1995 from the depreciation of the Canadian dollar. The fact that the depreciation did not lead to a persistent rise in inflation, even without a further tightening of monetary conditions, helped build the Bank's credibility.

35. The body of the *Monetary Policy Report* states, "Since the last *Report*, the Canadian economy has been weaker than expected and the degree of slack in labor and product markets has been correspondingly greater" (p. 3). And later, "Although a slowdown had been anticipated, the Bank was surprised (along with most others) by how abruptly the situation changed" (p. 6).

36. For example, "for the medium-term, a key issue is whether the trend of inflation might move below the 1 to 3 percent target range. . . . This in turn would imply an easing in the desired path of *medium-term* monetary conditions" (Bank of Canada 1996, May, p. 3). Governor Thiessen and other officers made similar statements to the press.

37. In addition to citing Akerlof, Dickens, and Perry (1996), Fortin also gives prominence to James Tobin's discussion of the macroeconomic significance of the nominal wage floor in his 1971 Presidential Address to the American Economic Association (p. 779).

38. See, for example, Crane (1996) and Fortin (1996b).

39. The speech, reprinted in Thiessen (1996a), was delivered before the Board of Trade of Metropolitan Toronto on November 6, 1996.

40. "However, inflation will work as a lubricant only if it fools people into believing that they are better off than they really are. There is, in fact, every reason to expect that people's behavior adapts to circumstances. In a low-inflation environment, employees are likely to

come to understand the need for occasional downward adjustments in wages or benefits" (Thiessen 1996a, pp. 68-9). Note that Thiessen does not assert that such wage flexibility has already occurred or is likely to arise quickly.

PART VI. UNITED KINGDOM

1. On May 6, 1997, the new Labour Chancellor of the Exchequer, Gordon Brown, announced that he was granting the Bank of England "operational independence," that is, the Bank could now set interest rates in the pursuit of the specified inflation goal at its own discretion. We return to this development at the end of this section.

2. This announcement was made official by the simultaneous delivery of a letter from the Chancellor to the Chairman of Parliament's Treasury and Civil Service Committee.

3. Speeches by officials of the Bank of Canada in the late 1980s leading up to that country's adoption of inflation targets made the same point with some of the same rhetorical spirit.

4. Of course, the Bank of England and the Chancellor were aware of the innovations in inflation targets in New Zealand and Canada, but, as typical and reasonable for national officials, explicit references in public to other countries' behavior were avoided. Still, the U.K adoption of inflation targeting may be legitimately thought of as part of a larger movement.

5. In a speech on June 14, 1995, Chancellor Kenneth Clarke (1995) announced that this objective would be extended indefinitely beyond the next general election. Without a change in the status of the Bank of England, however, the ruling party had no power with which to bind future governments, so the force of Clarke's statement was unclear. In late 1996, prior to the spring 1997 election campaign, Labour Party leaders indicated that they would continue the inflation-targeting framework (and the current targets) should they, as expected, win the election.

6. This is akin to the Swiss National Bank's rationale for its point target for monetary growth. As the Bank of England's own research suggests, however, if a target range were designed to truly capture some reasonable confidence interval of outcomes, given control problems, the range would be too wide for credibility with the general public. See Haldane and Salmon (1995).

7. Note that the point target does not imply performance assessment on the basis of a backward-looking average. Instead, the inflation performance relative to the point target is explained as the result of past actions and intervening developments. We are grateful to Mervyn King for clarifying this point.

8. The Labour Party's commitment to the inflation target and to greater operational independence for the Bank of England was made explicit in the party's official election platform. The rapid granting of independence—the day after Labour took office—nonetheless was a surprise to all observers.

9. The conveying of this information in an appropriate way to a nontechnical audience has challenged the staff of the *Inflation Report*. Initial efforts to depict the trend path of inflation with probability "cones" moving out from it were not widely understood. The recent pictures of a probability density for future inflation with shading from red (most likely) to pink (tail of distribution) appear to have been well received.

10. The statements quoted represent the Bank's official stance. In the same issue of the *Quarterly Bulletin*, the Bank's "General Assessment" echoes both statements—that "the achievement of price stability remained the ultimate objective of monetary policy" (p. 355), and that "had the United Kingdom remained in the ERM, it is quite possible that price stability would have been achieved during the next year. Although clearly desirable in itself, price stability attained too quickly might have intensified the problems of domestic debt deflation. Some easing of policy was, therefore, desirable" (p. 356).

11. At least, so long as an "optimal" contract for central bankers penalizing inflation performance alone is not in force.

12. There is some requirement for the Bank and its senior staff to give testimony to the House of Commons Treasury Committee, now on a regular basis as opposed to the by-request (though frequent) appearances in the past. Nonetheless, the record of these past testimonies—as well as the lack of incentives facing backbenchers on the committee to deviate from respective party leaderships' lines on monetary policy—suggests that these hearings are unlikely to influence Bank policy significantly.

13. The depreciation is measured by the Bank of England's exchange rate index.

14. The point should not be exaggerated, however, since Italy also managed to limit the pass-through effect of its ERM exit without adoption of inflation targets (see Laubach and Posen [1997b]).

15. See, for example, *Economist* (1994).

16. Minutes of the Monthly Monetary Meeting, July 28, 1994, p. 5.

17. Minutes of the Monthly Monetary Meeting, July 28, 1994, p. 6.

18. Svensson (1996) makes clear the benefits of having the transparent target be the monetary policymaker's inflation forecast.

19. The Bank assumes in its projections unchanged official interest rates and movements in the exchange rate reflecting the differential between U.K. and trade-weighted overseas short-term interest rates.

20. Several British press commentators observed that the timing of the May meeting was postponed until after some local elections, and took this as an indication that a rate hike was coming, since Clarke would not want to implement his policy the day before the polls. While the Bank-Chancellor meetings are monthly, the exact timing is not systematic, with occasional reschedulings occurring. In this instance, there was a widespread expectation before the meeting that the Chancellor would agree with the Bank's assessment; his later public overruling of the Bank, leaving rates unchanged, might be seen as an accommodation to broader Tory political reality, but one that emphasized the economic realities as well. As noted below, the U.K. press tends to look for politicization of monetary policy.

21. Minutes of the Monthly Monetary Meeting, June 7, 1995, p. 8.

22. Minutes of the Monthly Monetary Meeting, June 5, 1996, p. 9.

23. See, for example, *Financial Times* (1996). It should be noted that the British press tends to focus on the possibility that business and monetary cycles are governed by political and electoral developments, despite little econometric or other evidence to believe that such cycles are operative in the United Kingdom, an open economy with brief election campaigns on short notice.

24. Debelle and Fisher (1994) make the useful distinction between "goal" independence and "instrument" independence for central banks. For example, the Bundesbank has goal as well as instrument independence because it chooses inflation targets and sets interest rates. In the other three countries considered here, central banks have only instrument independence because the government, acting alone or jointly with the central bank, sets the goals of policy.

PART VII. HOW SUCCESSFUL HAS INFLATION TARGETING BEEN?

1. Ammer and Freeman (1995) perform a similar exercise. They interpret their results as showing below-predicted GDP growth after targeting, as well as lower inflation and interest rates. Their simulations, however, were based on data series ending two years before the series presented here. As can be seen in the GDP growth results for New Zealand and Canada (Panel B of Charts 2 and 3), GDP growth was initially below predicted values, perhaps due to the pre-adoption disinflationary policies. Over the whole post-targeting-adoption period, however, GDP growth rebounds and averages the predicted level.

For New Zealand, we use the discount rate because it is the only continuously available series that can be seen as reflecting the stance of monetary policy. Since the late 1980s, the Reserve Bank has been keeping the discount rate 0.9 percent above the interbank overnight rate.

2. A formal test for structural breaks in monetary policy reaction functions has three limitations that prevent its use in this assessment of inflation targeting's effectiveness: first, the test would be of extremely low power given the limited time since adoption even in New Zealand; second, the test would require us to impose a structural model of monetary policymaking for each country, which appears excessive; third, the test would provide a yes/no answer where more qualitative results are of interest.

3. Country-specific shocks are not the only potential source of problems for this comparison. Another possible reason why inflation and interest rates could be lower than forecast would be the existence of a widespread disinflationary trend across many countries over this time period, which drove these variables down in targeters and nontargeters alike. Laubach and Posen (1997b), however, explicitly compare the simulations for targeters and nontargeters over the same period and find that significant inflation and interest rate undershooting of forecast occurs only in the targeting countries.

4. Additional evidence suggests that the latter interpretation should be given more weight than the former. The effect of the adoption of inflation targeting on sacrifice ratios, or on the predictive power of previously estimated Phillips curves to continue forecasting inflation in the 1990s, appears to have been minimal, as mentioned at several points in the case studies.

REFERENCES

Abel, Andrew B., and Ben S. Bernanke. 1995. MACROECONOMICS. 2d ed. Reading, Mass.: Addison-Wesley Publishing Company.

Advisory Commission to Study the Consumer Price Index. 1996. "Toward a More Accurate Measure of the Cost of Living: Final Report to the Senate Finance Committee." Washington, D.C., December 4.

Akerlof, George, William Dickens, and George Perry. 1996. "The Macroeconomics of Low Inflation." BROOKINGS PAPERS ON ECONOMIC ACTIVITY, no. 1: 1-59.

Alesina, Alberto, and Lawrence H. Summers. 1993. "Central Bank Independence and Macroeconomic Performance: Some Comparative Evidence." JOURNAL OF MONEY, CREDIT, AND BANKING 25: 151-62.

Ammer, John, and Richard Freeman. 1995. "Inflation Targeting in the 1990s: The Experiences of New Zealand, Canada, and the United Kingdom." JOURNAL OF ECONOMICS AND BUSINESS 47 (May): 165-92.

Bailey, Martin J. 1956. "The Welfare Cost of Inflationary Finance." JOURNAL OF POLITICAL ECONOMY 64: 98-110.

Ball, Laurence. 1994. "What Determines the Sacrifice Ratio?" In N. Gregory Mankiw, ed., MONETARY POLICY. Chicago: University of Chicago Press.

Bank of Canada. 1991-96a. ANNUAL REPORT, various issues.

———. 1991b. "Targets for Reducing Inflation: Announcements and Background Material." BANK OF CANADA REVIEW, March: 3-21.

———. 1991c. "Targets for Reducing Inflation: Further Operational and Measurement Considerations." BANK OF CANADA REVIEW, September: 3-23.

———. 1993-94. "Statement of the Government of Canada and the Bank of Canada on Monetary Policy Objectives." BANK OF CANADA REVIEW, winter: 85-6.

———. 1995-97. MONETARY POLICY REPORT, various issues.

Bank of England. 1992-96. BANK OF ENGLAND INFLATION REPORT, various issues.

Barro, Robert J. 1993. MACROECONOMICS. 4th ed. New York: John Wiley & Sons.

———. 1995. "Inflation and Economic Growth." BANK OF ENGLAND QUARTERLY BULLETIN 35 (May): 166-76.

Barro, Robert J., and David Gordon. 1983. "A Positive Theory of Monetary Policy in a Natural Rate Model." JOURNAL OF POLITICAL ECONOMY 91: 589-610.

Bernanke, Ben S., and Ilian Mihov. 1997. "What Does the Bundesbank Target?" EUROPEAN ECONOMIC REVIEW 41, no. 6 (June): 1025-53.

Bernanke, Ben S., and Frederic S. Mishkin. 1992. "Central Bank Behavior and the Strategy of Monetary Policy: Observations from Six Industrialized Countries." In Olivier Blanchard and Stanley Fischer, eds., NBER MACROECONOMICS ANNUAL, 1992. Cambridge: MIT Press.

———. 1997. "Inflation Targeting: A New Framework for Monetary Policy?" JOURNAL OF ECONOMIC PERSPECTIVES 11, no. 2 (spring): 97-116.

Birch, W.F. 1996. "NZ Monetary and Fiscal Policy Consistent and Has Reserve Bank Support." FINANCIAL TIMES, letter to the editor, January 9, p. 12.

Brash, Donald T. 1996a. "Address to the Auckland Manufacturers' Association." February.

———. 1996b. "New Zealand's Remarkable Reforms." The Fifth IEA Annual Hayek Memorial Lecture. Institute of Economic Affairs Occasional Paper no. 100.

———. 1997. "Address to the Canterbury Employers' Chamber of Commerce." January.

Briault, Clive. 1995. "The Costs of Inflation." BANK OF ENGLAND QUARTERLY BULLETIN 35 (February): 33-45.

Bruno, Michael, and William Easterly. 1995. "Inflation Crises and Long-Run Growth." NBER Working Paper no. 5209.

Bryant, Ralph. 1996. "Central Bank Independence, Fiscal Responsibility, and the Goals of Macroeconomic Policy: An American Perspective on the New Zealand Experience." Unpublished paper, Victoria University of Wellington, May.

Calvo, Guillermo. 1978. "On the Time Consistency of Optimal Policy in the Monetary Economy." ECONOMETRICA 46: 1411-28.

Capie, Forrest, et al. 1994. THE FUTURE OF CENTRAL BANKING: THE TERCENTENARY SYMPOSIUM OF THE BANK OF ENGLAND. Cambridge: Cambridge University Press.

REFERENCES *(Continued)*

Carey, David. 1989. "Inflation and the Tax System." RESERVE BANK OF NEW ZEALAND BULLETIN 52, no. 1 (March): 18-26.

Chote, Robert. 1997. "Treading the Line between Credibility and Humility." FINANCIAL TIMES, June 13, p. 9.

Chote, Robert, Phillip Coggan, and Robert Peston. 1995. "Pound Hit as Clarke Fails to Lift Rates." FINANCIAL TIMES, May 6-7, p. 1.

Clarida, Richard, and Mark Gertler. 1997. "How the Bundesbank Conducts Monetary Policy." In Christina D. Romer and David H. Romer, eds., REDUCING INFLATION: MOTIVATION AND STRATEGY, 363-406. Chicago: University of Chicago Press.

Clarke, Kenneth. 1995. Mansion House Speech to the City, June 14. Excerpted in FINANCIAL TIMES, June 15, p. 10.

Coote, Michael. 1996. "Price Stability Requires a Tight, Not Loose, Inflation Target." NEW ZEALAND BUSINESS REVIEW, p. 70.

Cozier, Barry, and Gordon Wilkinson. 1991. "Some Evidence on Hysteresis and the Costs of Disinflation in Canada." Bank of Canada Technical Report no. 55.

Crane, David. 1993. "John Crow Deserves to Be Fired, Not Rehired." TORONTO STAR, November 14, p. D4.

———. 1996. "Bank of Canada Should Rethink Zero Inflation." TORONTO STAR, September 5.

Crow, John W. 1988. "The Work of Canadian Monetary Policy." The Hanson Lecture. BANK OF CANADA REVIEW, February: 3-17.

———. 1989. "Targeting Monetary Policy." BANK OF CANADA REVIEW, December: 21-8.

———. 1990. "Current Monetary Policy." BANK OF CANADA REVIEW, September: 33-41.

———. 1991a. "General Observations." BANK OF CANADA ANNUAL REPORT, 1990: 7-12.

———. 1991b. "Method and Myth in Monetary Policy." BANK OF CANADA REVIEW, July: 9-14.

Cukierman, Alex. 1992. CENTRAL BANK STRATEGY, CREDIBILITY, AND INDEPENDENCE: THEORY AND EVIDENCE. Cambridge: MIT Press.

Debelle, Guy, and Stanley Fischer. 1994. "How Independent Should a Central Bank Be?" In Jeffrey C. Fuhrer, ed., GOALS, GUIDELINES, AND CONSTRAINTS FACING MONETARY POLICYMAKERS. Federal Reserve Bank of Boston Conference Series 38: 195-221.

Deutsche Bundesbank. 1974-96a. ANNUAL REPORT, various issues.

———. 1974-96b. MONTHLY REPORT, various issues.

———. 1995c. THE MONETARY POLICY OF THE BUNDESBANK. October.

Dornbusch, Rudiger, and Stanley Fischer. 1994. MACROECONOMICS. 6th ed. New York: McGraw-Hill.

Easton, Brian. 1994. "Economic and Other Ideas Behind the New Zealand Reforms." OXFORD REVIEW OF ECONOMIC POLICY 10, no. 3: 78-94.

Economist. 1994. "Willkommen Herr Clarke." September 17.

English, William B. 1996. "Inflation and Financial Sector Size." Board of Governors of the Federal Reserve System Finance and Economics Discussion Series, no. 96-16, April.

Fallow, Brian. 1996. "Wider Inflation Target Is Risky Policy—Brash." NEW ZEALAND HERALD, June 28.

Feldstein, Martin. 1997. "The Costs and Benefits of Going from Low Inflation to Price Stability." In Christina D. Romer and David H. Romer, eds., REDUCING INFLATION: MOTIVATION AND STRATEGY, 123-56. Chicago: University of Chicago Press.

Financial Times. 1996. "Shares Hit as Rates Rise to 6%." October 31.

Fischer, Andreas M., and Adrian B. Orr. 1994. "Monetary Policy Credibility and Price Uncertainty: The New Zealand Experience of Inflation Targeting." OECD ECONOMIC STUDIES 22 (spring): 155-79.

Fischer, Stanley. 1981. "Towards an Understanding of the Costs of Inflation: II." CARNEGIE-ROCHESTER CONFERENCE SERIES ON PUBLIC POLICY 15: 5-41.

———. 1987. "Monetary Policy and Performance in the U.S., Japan, and Europe, 1973-86." In Y. Suzuki and M. Okabe, eds., TOWARD A WORLD OF ECONOMIC STABILITY: OPTIMAL MONETARY FRAMEWORK AND POLICY. Tokyo: University of Tokyo Press.

REFERENCES (*Continued*)

———. 1991. "Growth, Macroeconomics, and Development." In NBER MACROECONOMICS ANNUAL, 1991, 329-79. Cambridge: MIT Press.

———. 1993. "The Role of Macroeconomic Factors in Growth." JOURNAL OF MONETARY ECONOMICS 32: 485-512.

———. 1994. "Modern Central Banking." In Forrest Capie et al., THE FUTURE OF CENTRAL BANKING: THE TERCENTENARY SYMPOSIUM OF THE BANK OF ENGLAND. Cambridge: Cambridge University Press.

———. 1995. "Modern Approaches to Central Banking." NBER Working Paper no. 5064, March.

Fortin, Pierre. 1996a. "The Great Canadian Slump." CANADIAN JOURNAL OF ECONOMICS 29, no. 4 (November): 761-87.

———. 1996b. "Raise the Inflation Target and Let Canada Recover." GLOBE AND MAIL, September 26.

Freedman, Charles. 1994a. "Formal Targets for Inflation Reduction: The Canadian Experience." In J. Wijnholds, S. Eijffinger, and L. Hoogduin, eds., A FRAMEWORK FOR MONETARY STABILITY. Dordrecht and Boston: Kluwer Academic.

———. 1994b. "The Use of Indicators and of the Monetary Conditions Index in Canada." In T. Balino and C. Cottarelli, eds., FRAMEWORKS FOR MONETARY STABILITY: POLICY ISSUES AND COUNTRY EXPERIENCES. Washington, D.C.: International Monetary Fund.

———. 1995. "The Canadian Experience with Targets for Reducing and Controlling Inflation." In Leonardo Leiderman and Lars E.O. Svensson, eds., INFLATION TARGETS, 19-31. London: Centre for Economic Policy Research.

Freeman, Richard, and John Willis. 1995. "Targeting Inflation in the 1990s: Recent Challenges." Board of Governors of the Federal Reserve System International Finance Discussion Papers, no. 525.

Friedman, Benjamin M. 1995. "The Rise and Fall of the Money Growth Targets as Guidelines for U.S. Monetary Policy." Paper prepared for the Bank of Japan Seventh International Conference. Preliminary draft.

Friedman, Benjamin M., and Kenneth Kuttner. 1996. "A Price Target for U.S. Monetary Policy? Lessons from the Experience with Money Growth Targets." BROOKINGS PAPERS ON ECONOMIC ACTIVITY, no. 1: 77-125.

Friedman, Milton. 1968. "The Role of Monetary Policy." AMERICAN ECONOMIC REVIEW 58: 1-17.

Fuhrer, Jeffrey C. 1995. "The Phillips Curve Is Alive and Well." Federal Reserve Bank of Boston NEW ENGLAND ECONOMIC REVIEW, March-April: 41-56.

George, Eddie. 1995a. "Monetary Policy Realities." BANK OF ENGLAND QUARTERLY BULLETIN 35, no. 4 (November): 388-94.

———. 1995b. "The Prospects for Monetary Stability." Speech to the City, June 14. Reprint, BANK OF ENGLAND QUARTERLY BULLETIN 35, no. 3 (August): 295-6.

Goodhart, Charles A.E. 1981. "Problems in Monetary Management: the UK Experience." In A.S. Courakis, ed., INFLATION, DEPRESSION AND ECONOMIC POLICY IN THE WEST. Totowa, N.J.: Barnes and Noble.

Goodhart, Charles A.E., and José Viñals. 1995. "Strategy and Tactics of Monetary Policy: Examples from Europe and the Antipodes." In Jeffrey C. Fuhrer, ed., GOALS, GUIDELINES, AND CONSTRAINTS FACING MONETARY POLICYMAKERS. Federal Reserve Bank of Boston Conference Series 38: 139-87.

Gordon, Robert R. 1985. "Understanding Inflation in the 1980's." BROOKINGS PAPERS ON ECONOMIC ACTIVITY, no. 1: 263-302.

Groshen, Erica L., and Mark E. Schweitzer. 1996. "The Effects of Inflation on Wage Adjustments in Firm-Level Data: Grease or Sand?" Federal Reserve Bank of New York Staff Reports, no. 9.

Haldane, Andrew G.,s and Christopher K. Salmon. 1995. "Three Issues on Inflation Targets." In Andrew G. Haldane, ed., TARGETING INFLATION, 170-201. London: Bank of England.

Hall, Robert E., and John B. Taylor. 1993. MACROECONOMICS. 4th ed. New York: W.W. Norton and Company.

Hall, Terry. 1995. "NZ Bank Chief Admits Price Rise Slippage." FINANCIAL TIMES, June 30, p. 6.

———. 1996a. "NZ Central Bank Hints at Monetary Easing." FINANCIAL TIMES, October 25, p. 6.

———. 1996b. "NZ Bank Cautious on Wider Inflation Target." FINANCIAL TIMES, December 18, p. 8.

Hansen, Lars Peter, and Robert J. Hodrick. 1980. "Forward Exchange Rates as Optimal Predictors of Future Spot Rates: An Econometric Analysis." JOURNAL OF POLITICAL ECONOMY 88: 829-53.

Hefeker, Carsten. 1994. "German Monetary Union, the Bundesbank, and the EMS Collapse." BANCA NATIONAL DEL LAVORO QUARTERLY REVIEW 47 (December): 379-98.

Hess, Gregory D., and Charles S. Morris. 1996. "The Long-Run Costs of Moderate Inflation." Federal Reserve Bank of Kansas City ECONOMIC REVIEW, second quarter: 71-88.

House Joint Resolution no. 409. 1989. 101st Cong., 1st sess.

Huh, Chan. 1996. "Some Evidence on the Efficacy of the UK Inflation Targeting Regime: An Out-of-Sample Forecast Approach." Board of Governors of the Federal Reserve System International Finance Discussion Papers, no. 565.

Hutchison, Michael M., and Carl E. Walsh. 1996. "Central Bank Institutional Design and the Output Cost of Disinflation: Did the 1989 New Zealand Reserve Bank Act Affect the Inflation-Output Tradeoff?" Reserve Bank of New Zealand Research Paper G96/6.

Ip, Greg. 1991. "Inflation War is Won, Bank of Canada Says." FINANCIAL POST, October 15, p. 40.

———. 1993. "Drop in Inflation Rate Beats Expectations." FINANCIAL POST, December 8, p. 5.

Issing, Otmar. 1995a. "Monetary Policy in an Integrated World Economy." Unpublished paper, University of Kiel, June.

———. 1995b. "The Relationship Between the Constancy of Monetary Policy and the Stability of the Monetary System." Paper presented at the Gerzensee Symposium of the Swiss National Bank.

Jenkins, W. 1990. "The Goal of Price Stability." BANK OF CANADA REVIEW, July: 3-7.

Judson, Ruth, and Athanasios Orphanides. 1996. "Inflation, Volatility, and Growth." Unpublished paper, Board of Governors of the Federal Reserve System, May.

König, Reiner, and Caroline Willeke. 1996. "German Monetary Reunification." CENTRAL BANKING, May: 29-39.

Kydland, Fin, and Edward Prescott. 1977. "Rules Rather than Discretion: The Inconsistency of Optimal Plans." JOURNAL OF POLITICAL ECONOMY 85: 473-92.

Laidler, David, and William Robson. 1993. THE GREAT CANADIAN DISINFLATION. Montreal: C. D. Howe Research Institute.

Lamont, Norman. 1992. Mansion House Speech to the City, October 29. Reprint, FINANCIAL TIMES, October 30, p. 14.

Laubach, Thomas, and Adam S. Posen. 1997a. "Disciplined Discretion: The German and Swiss Monetary Frameworks in Operation." Federal Reserve Bank of New York Research Paper no. 9707, March.

———. 1997b. "Some Comparative Evidence on the Effectiveness of Inflation Targeting." Federal Reserve Bank of New York Research Paper no. 9714, May.

Leigh-Pemberton, Robin. 1984. "Some Aspects of UK Monetary Policy." BANK OF ENGLAND QUARTERLY BULLETIN 24, no. 4 (December): 474-81.

———. 1990. "Some Remarks on Exchange Rate Regimes." BANK OF ENGLAND QUARTERLY BULLETIN 30, no. 4 (November): 482-4.

———. 1991. "Stability and Economic Policy." BANK OF ENGLAND QUARTERLY BULLETIN 31, no. 4 (November): 496-7.

———. 1992. "The Case for Price Stability." London School of Economics–Bank of England Lecture, presented on November 11, 1992. Reprint, BANK OF ENGLAND QUARTERLY BULLETIN 32, no. 4 (November): 441-8.

Lloyd, Michele. 1992. "The New Zealand Approach to Central Bank Autonomy." RESERVE BANK OF NEW ZEALAND BULLETIN 55, no. 3: 203-20.

Longworth, David, and Charles Freedman. 1995. "The Role of the Staff Economic Projection in Conducting Canadian Monetary Policy." In A. Haldane, ed., TARGETING INFLATION, 101-12. London: Bank of England.

Louisson, Simon. 1994. "New Zealand Inflation May Burst Target." Reuters World Service, December 6.

Mankiw, N. Gregory. 1994. MACROECONOMICS. 2d ed. New York: Worth Publishers.

Marotte, Bertrand. 1993. "Markets Endorse New Governor: Central Bank to Continue Inflation Battle." OTTAWA CITIZEN, December 23, p. D6.

Marsh, David. 1992. THE BUNDESBANK. London: William Heinemann.

McCallum, Bennett T. 1995a. "Inflation Targeting in Canada, New Zealand, Sweden, and the United Kingdom, and in General." Paper prepared for the Bank of Japan Seventh International Conference. Preliminary draft.

REFERENCES (*Continued*)

———. 1995b. "Two Fallacies Concerning Central-Bank Independence." AMERICAN ECONOMIC REVIEW 85, no. 2 (May): 207-11. Papers and Proceedings of the 107th Annual Meeting of the American Economic Association, Washington, D.C., January 6-8.

McDonough, William J. 1996a. "A Strategy for Monetary Policy." Speech given before the Annual Financial Services Forum of the New York State Bankers Association, New York, N.Y., March 21.

———. 1996b. "The Importance of Price Stability." Speech given before the Economic Club of New York, New York, N.Y., October 2.

McGillivray, Don. 1994. "Bank Still Headed in Wrong Direction." CALGARY HERALD, January 4, p. A4.

Meek, Paul, ed. 1983. CENTRAL BANK VIEWS ON MONETARY TARGETING. New York: Federal Reserve Bank of New York.

Mishkin, Frederic S. 1994. ECONOMICS OF MONEY, BANKING AND FINANCIAL MARKETS. 4th ed. New York: HarperCollins.

———. 1996. "Understanding Financial Crises: A Developing Country Perspective." In Michael Bruno and Boris Pleskovic, eds., ANNUAL WORLD BANK CONFERENCE ON DEVELOPMENT ECONOMICS, 1996, 29-62. Washington, D.C.: World Bank.

———. 1997. "Strategies for Controlling Inflation." In Reserve Bank of Australia, MONETARY POLICY AND INFLATION TARGETING. Forthcoming.

Montagnon, Peter. 1995. "Bank Governor Passes First Inflation Test." FINANCIAL TIMES, October 22, p. 4.

Neumann, Manfred. 1996. "Monetary Targeting in Germany." Paper prepared for the Bank of Japan Seventh International Conference.

Neumann, Manfred J.M., and Jurgen von Hagen. 1993. "Germany." In M. Fratianni and D. Salvatore, eds., HANDBOOK OF MONETARY POLICY IN INDUSTRIALIZED COUNTRIES. Westport, Conn.: Greenwood.

New Zealand Herald. 1990a. "Pressure on Government to Relax Inflation Target." August 4.

———. 1990b. "Most Voters Back Target of Lower Inflation." October 25.

Nicholl, Peter W.E., and David J. Archer. 1992. "An Announced Downward Path for Inflation." In Richard O'Brien, ed., FINANCE AND THE INTERNATIONAL ECONOMY, no. 6. Oxford: Oxford University Press. Reprint, RESERVE BANK OF NEW ZEALAND BULLETIN, December.

Obstfeld, Maurice, and Kenneth Rogoff. 1995. "The Mirage of Fixed Exchange Rates." JOURNAL OF ECONOMIC PERSPECTIVES 9, no. 4 (fall).

Posen, Adam S. 1995. "Central Bank Independence and Disinflationary Credibility: A Missing Link?" Federal Reserve Bank of New York Staff Reports, no. 1, May.

Reddell, Michael. 1988. "Inflation and the Monetary Policy Strategy." RESERVE BANK OF NEW ZEALAND BULLETIN 51, no. 2 (June): 81-4.

Reserve Bank of New Zealand. 1985a. "Reserve Bank Annual Report." RESERVE BANK OF NEW ZEALAND BULLETIN 48, no. 8 (August): 446-54.

———. 1985b. "The Functions of the Reserve Bank." RESERVE BANK OF NEW ZEALAND BULLETIN 48, no. 9 (September): 512-3.

———. 1987. "A Layman's Guide to Monetary Policy in the New Zealand Context." RESERVE BANK OF NEW ZEALAND BULLETIN 50 (June): 104-10.

———. 1990. RESERVE BANK OF NEW ZEALAND BULLETIN 53, no. 1 (March).

———. 1991. MONETARY POLICY STATEMENT. August.

———. 1992a. MONETARY POLICY STATEMENT. February.

———. 1992b. MONETARY POLICY STATEMENT. June.

———. 1995. MONETARY POLICY STATEMENT. December.

Reuters Financial Service. 1991. "Lower NZ Dollar Not a Threat to Inflation—Bolger." October 24.

Roll, Eric, et al. 1993. INDEPENDENT AND ACCOUNTABLE: A NEW MANDATE FOR THE BANK OF ENGLAND. London: Centre for Economic Policy Research.

Sarel, Michael. 1996. "Nonlinear Effects of Inflation on Economic Growth." IMF STAFF PAPERS 43 (March): 199-215.

Schlesinger, Helmut. 1983. "The Setting of Monetary Objectives in Germany." In Paul Meek, ed., CENTRAL BANK VIEWS ON MONETARY TARGETING. Federal Reserve Bank of New York.

Schmid, Peter. 1996. "Monetary Policy: Targets and Instruments." CENTRAL BANKING, May: 40-51.

REFERENCES *(Continued)*

Shapiro, Matthew D., and David W. Wilcox. 1996. "Causes and Consequences of Imperfections in the Consumer Price Index." In Ben S. Bernanke and Julio J. Rotemberg, eds., NBER MACROECONOMICS ANNUAL, 1996. Cambridge: MIT Press.

Stevens, Glenn, and Guy Debelle. 1995. "Monetary Policy Goals for Inflation in Australia." In Andrew G. Haldane, ed., TARGETING INFLATION, 81-100. London: Bank of England.

Svensson, Lars. 1993. "The Simplest Test of Target Credibility." NBER Working Paper no. 4604.

———. 1996. "Inflation Forecast Targeting: Implementing and Monitoring Inflation Targets." NBER Working Paper no. 5797, October.

Szep, Jason. 1991. "Canada Plans to Introduce Inflation-Indexed Bonds." Reuters Financial Service, May 28.

Tait, Nikki. 1995. "NZ Bank Chief Sticks to Policy." FINANCIAL TIMES, May 3.

———. 1996. "NZ Deal Gives Rise to Faith and Doubt." FINANCIAL TIMES, December 20.

Taylor, John B. 1995. "The Inflation/Output Variability Trade-off Revisited." In Jeffrey C. Fuhrer, ed., GOALS, GUIDELINES, AND CONSTRAINTS FACING MONETARY POLICYMAKERS, 21-38. Federal Reserve Bank of Boston Conference Series 38.

Thiessen, Gordon. 1991. "Notes for Remarks by Gordon G. Thiessen, Senior Deputy Governor of the Bank of Canada." BANK OF CANADA REVIEW, July: 15-21.

———. 1994a. "Further Direction for the Bank of Canada and Monetary Policy." BANK OF CANADA REVIEW, spring: 85-90.

———. 1994b. "Opening Statement before the Standing Senate Committee on Banking, Trade, and Commerce." BANK OF CANADA REVIEW, spring: 81-90.

———. 1995a. "Notes for Remarks to the Winnipeg Chamber of Commerce."

———. 1995b. "Opening Statement before the Standing Senate Committee on Banking, Trade, and Commerce." BANK OF CANADA REVIEW, spring: 85-8.

———. 1995c. "Statement from the Governor." BANK OF CANADA ANNUAL REPORT, 1995: 5-8.

———. 1995d. "Uncertainty and the Transmission of Monetary Policy in Canada." The Hermes-Gordon Lecture. BANK OF CANADA REVIEW, summer: 41-58.

———. 1996a. "Does Canada Need More Inflation to Grease the Wheels of the Economy?" BANK OF CANADA REVIEW, winter: 47-62.

———. 1996b. "Monetary Policy and the Canadian Economy in a Changing World." The Siebens Lecture.

———. 1996c. "Statement from the Governor." BANK OF CANADA ANNUAL REPORT, 1995: 5-8.

———. 1996d. "Towards a More Transparent and More Credible Monetary Policy." Remarks delivered at the Ecole des Hautes Etudes Commerciales.

Vardy, Jill. 1993. "Crow Out, Thiessen In: New Bank of Canada Governor Will Continue Inflation-Fighting Policies." FINANCIAL POST, December 23, p. 1.

von Hagen, Jurgen. 1995. "Inflation and Monetary Targeting in Germany." In Leonardo Leiderman and Lars E.O. Svensson, eds., INFLATION TARGETS. London: Centre for Economic Policy Research.

Walsh, Carl E. 1995. "Rules vs. Discretion in New Zealand Monetary Policy." Federal Reserve Bank of San Francisco ECONOMIC LETTER, no. 95-09 (March 3).

———. 1996. "Accountability in Practice: Recent Monetary Policy in New Zealand." Federal Reserve Bank of San Francisco ECONOMIC LETTER, no. 96-25 (September 9).